YOU CAN BE AN ACTIVIST

HOW TO USE YOUR STRENGTHS & PASSIONS TO MAKE A DIFFERENCE

WRITTEN BY
CHARLENE ROCHA
AND
MARY BETH LEATHERDALE

ILLUSTRATED BY
DREW SHANNON

Citizen **Kid**™

A collection of books that inform
children about the world and
inspire them to be engaged
global citizens

Kids Can Press

For the dreamers and the doers who will build
a better world — Charlene and Mary Beth

Published in Canada and the U.S. by Kids Can Press Ltd.
25 Dockside Drive, Toronto, ON M5A 0B5

Kids Can Press is a Corus Entertainment Inc. company

www.kidscanpress.com

The artwork in this book was rendered digitally.
The text is set in Lazy Dog, Londrina and Open Sans.

Edited by Kathleen Keenan
Designed by Andrew Dupuis

Printed and bound in Buji, Shenzhen, China, in 3/2024 by WKT Company

CM 24 0 9 8 7 6 5 4 3 2 1

LIBRARY AND ARCHIVES CANADA CATALOGUING IN PUBLICATION

Title: You can be an activist : how to use your strengths and passions to make a difference /
written by Charlene Rocha and Mary Beth Leatherdale ; illustrated by Drew Shannon.
Names: Rocha, Charlene, author. | Leatherdale, Mary Beth, author. | Shannon, Drew, 1988– illustrator.
Series: CitizenKid.
Description: Series statement: CitizenKid | Includes index.
Identifiers: Canadiana (print) 20230571190 | Canadiana (ebook) 20240301668 |
ISBN 9781525308406 (softcover) | ISBN 9781525312694 (EPUB)
Subjects: LCSH: Activism — Juvenile literature. | LCSH: Social justice — Juvenile literature. |
LCSH: Social action — Juvenile literature. | LCSH: Children — Political activity — Juvenile literature. |
LCGFT: Instructional and educational works.
Classification: LCC HM671 .R59 2024 | DDC j303.3/72 — dc23

Kids Can Press gratefully acknowledges that the land on which our office is located is the traditional
territory of many nations, including the Mississaugas of the Credit, the Anishnabeg, the Chippewa,
the Haudenosaunee and the Wendat peoples, and is now home to many diverse First Nations, Inuit
and Métis peoples.

We thank the Government of Ontario, through Ontario Creates and the Ontario Arts Council; the
Canada Council for the Arts; and the Government of Canada for their financial support of our
publishing activity.

TABLE OF CONTENTS

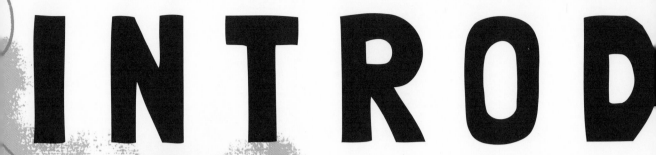

INTROD

Our world is not perfect. But thankfully, there is a lot that we can do to change it for the better. Sometimes, when we witness or experience something that's unfair, we feel an urge to take action. I felt this when I was the only girl in my robotics class and wondered why more girls weren't encouraged to pursue engineering fields. I feel it when I witness something beautiful in nature, only to realize climate change may prevent other generations from seeing that beauty. I feel it when I learn about systemic racism and speak with my Black peers about their experiences of discrimination. I feel it when I appreciate the land I live on as a second-generation immigrant and reflect on the Indigenous Nations that have had their lands stolen. Activism gives us the opportunity to act on these and other social justice issues. With every ripple effect created by our activism, we can slowly but surely make a better future.

Although I wanted to act on the passions I was feeling, I was always a little hesitant to get involved. Looking at climate activists

UCTION

portrayed in the media, I didn't see many people of color like me and assumed that activism wasn't "my thing." I was scared that I was too shy, didn't have anything to bring to the table or didn't know enough to get started ... and I was very wrong! As I began volunteering more in my community by joining my school's 2SLGBTQIA+ rights group, Alliance for Compassion, attending Fridays for Future climate action strikes and making connections with local activists, I slowly built my confidence. Through these experiences, I finally felt surrounded by a group of like-minded, passionate people.

Activism can sound intimidating initially, but it's welcoming to all who are looking to learn and make a difference! There is no set list of requirements for what you need to help others and make change in your community. Absolutely anyone can do it.

I've learned so much from my experiences as an activist. And I want to share with you the things I've learned and the tools I've developed. But the ideas that you find in this book reflect just one perspective — mine.

Other activists you meet will have their own ideas and insights. And on your activism journey, you'll develop your own.

Whether you're looking to find your passion, join a group or start a movement, your unique talents and perspectives are needed! We're all stronger together and our diverse abilities can have a significant impact. I can't wait to see how you change the world!

— Charlene

1

YOU CAN BE AN
ACTIVIST

One chilly spring day, my older sister and I bundled up in winter gear and headed down to the Legislative Assembly of Ontario to participate in our first Fridays for Future climate action strike. The Legislative Assembly is where members of the provincial government meet. I had been a student page there two years before, delivering messages for politicians and learning about the government. Pages were able to observe debates on topics involving our communities but weren't allowed to discuss or share our own opinions on any of the issues. But this day was different. Young people were there, speaking passionately about how to stop climate change as hundreds of shivering protesters applauded and cheered. I was so inspired that I jumped up and asked the organizers if I could speak. Trying my best to ignore the wall of news cameras pointed at me, I grabbed the mic and spoke from my heart, sharing my fear, anger and despair about what humans are doing to the environment. I confided that being surrounded by young people taking action gave me hope that we could overcome the climate crisis. In that very moment, as if I was watching myself in a dream, I realized that I was an activist and part of an incredible community. And I've been working for social change ever since!

WHAT IS AN ACTIVIST?

Still, in North America and around the world, inequality and injustice run rampant. The fight is not over. As people in the past did for us, we need to fight for our generation and the generations to come. We have the responsibility and the privilege to create a peaceful, united world.

Many of you are already activists and don't know it. If you've ever joined an eco team, raised money for a charity, volunteered at a food bank or helped an elderly neighbor, you've acted for social change — and that's activism! You see, activists aren't just well-known people like Greta Thunberg or Malala Yousafzai. In fact, most of the important activism work is done out of the spotlight by people you've never heard of — or never will. Thanks to many unsung activists of the past, my parents were able to immigrate to Canada from India, I am able to vote as a woman, I have the right to express my opinions publicly and I can go to school to get an education.

ACTIVIST:

Someone who stands up for their own rights and the rights of others, taking action to create social change that benefits other people and the planet.

QUIET ACTIONS = BIG IMPACT

Marching and demonstrating aren't the only ways to fight for social change. You may be more of a quiet activist. Quiet activists are just as passionate about changing society for the better. But they're more comfortable supporting social justice issues with thoughtful actions, collaboration and creativity. Everything from helping a refugee family settle into their new home to cleaning up litter in your neighborhood can be a political act. So can writing a letter or a protest song. Plus, your quiet approach to activism may be less intimidating to some people, so they may be more open to getting involved. (See how the Craftivist Collective made big change quietly on page 89.)

MYTH	REALITY
Activists work to help others, not themselves.	Supporting the community you're in or acting to change an injustice you may experience personally is also activism. The cause you're passionate about can include issues that you, a friend or someone else in your community faces.
All activists have to be good at public speaking.	You don't have to be on camera to make change. The people behind the scenes who organize events, make posters, create social media campaigns and more are doing important work, too. (And remember, it's normal to get nervous when you're speaking in public!)
Activists need to know everything about the cause they're fighting for.	Activism is a learning process. Keep educating yourself, but recognize that it takes time to acquire a deep understanding of an issue. The most important thing is to keep learning.
Activists must be adults.	You can start taking action at any age. It is *never* too late or too early.

CHANGEMAKERS

In 1965, the Vietnam War was raging. Mary Beth Tinker, a junior high student in Des Moines, Iowa, was upset that thousands of civilians and Vietnamese and American soldiers were being killed in the fighting. So, she, her siblings and some friends decided to wear black armbands to school to raise awareness about the war. Mary Beth and others were suspended for their protest. But their small, quiet action had a huge impact. These young anti-war activists challenged their school's ban against armbands in court. After a four-year legal battle, the Supreme Court ruled that students' constitutional rights to freedom of speech or expression were protected at school. Since then, thanks to these peaceful protesters, American students are able to raise their voices and advocate for change at school.

THE
PEOPLE
HAVE THE
POWER

Even though I always cared about social justice and wanted to have a positive impact on the world, I didn't know where to start. I participated in school clubs, did litter pickups with community organizations and volunteered whenever I could, but I wanted to do *more*. I worried that I was starting "too late" to have a larger impact or that I didn't have anything unique to contribute. It wasn't until my sister and I went to a Fridays for Future strike that I understood that my actions *could* make a difference. Rather than just sitting around and hoping my insecurities about being an imperfect activist would go away, I decided I wanted to be part of these movements and started learning!

So, what are some of the challenges that exist around the globe today? And who's going to fix them? We are! As activists, we need to understand the problems and educate ourselves on what we can do to help. We don't need to be afraid of each other, and we don't need to be afraid of the future. What solutions do you want to be part of?

TAKE ACTION

The United Nations has put together a blueprint to achieve a better and more sustainable future for all. The UN Sustainable Development Goals focus on tackling 17 of the world's biggest social justice issues. And you can help!

Goal 1: No Poverty. Encourage your family to buy fair trade chocolate to make sure farmers and laborers are paid a living wage.

Goal 2: Zero Hunger. Help out at a food bank.

Goal 3: Good Health and Well-Being. Make sure you have all your recommended vaccinations.

Goal 4: Quality Education. Volunteer to be a peer tutor.

Goal 5: Gender Equality. Urge your school to make period products available for students at no cost.

Goal 6: Clean Water and Sanitation. Create posters about the right to clean water and put them up at your school.

Goal 7: Affordable and Clean Energy. Ask your family to use only energy efficient light bulbs.

Goal 8: Decent Work and Economic Growth. Use your purchasing power to support young entrepreneurs.

Goal 9: Industry, Innovation and Infrastructure. Write your government to lobby for equal broadband internet access in your country.

Goal 10: Reduced Inequalities. Speak up when you hear classmates or family members use stereotypes.

Goal 11: Sustainable Cities and Communities. Whenever possible, bike or use public transit.

Goal 12: Responsible Consumption and Production. Participate in Zero Waste Week.

Goal 13: Climate Action. Walk to school instead of being driven.

Goal 14: Life Below Water. Refuse, reduce and reuse plastic.

Goal 15: Life on Land. Swap out meat for plant-based foods.

Goal 16: Peace, Justice and Strong Institutions. Collect toys and books to donate to organizations supporting refugees and newcomers in your community.

Goal 17: Partnerships for the Goals. Suggest your family lend money to support small businesses through a microloans platform like Kiva.org instead of buying you birthday presents.

Source: Sustainable Development Goals, United Nations

YOU'VE GOT WHAT IT TAKES

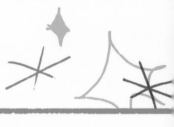

So do you have what it takes to be an activist? You bet you do! But before you get started, you need to understand why you want to do this. Every activist has a *why* — the reason they do what they do. Your *why* isn't about a particular goal, such as organizing a protest or the number of reposts you get. Those things should support your *why* but they don't define it. What is it that drives you?

SO YOU WANT TO BE AN ACTIVIST

1. **Why** do you want to do this?
2. **Who** are you trying to help?
3. **What** social change are you fighting for?
4. **Why** is this issue meaningful to you?
5. **Why** does this issue need to be resolved?
6. **How** are you going to help?
7. **Who** can help you?
8. **How** do you get started?

Remember to consider your unique strengths and personality while setting your activism goals. Talents like playing an instrument or drawing may be easier to identify than being good at teamwork or able to quickly learn how to use apps and software. But it's pooling our diverse strengths and passions that allows us to build a strong team and get the work done. Whether your gift is designing posters to raise awareness or creating a database to track potential supporters, you're helping your cause.

USE YOUR STRENGTHS AND PASSIONS TO SET YOUR ACTIVISM GOALS.

For example, you can put your math whiz skills to work by planning a cookie sale to raise funds for an animal rescue organization. How much will each cookie cost? How many cookies do you need to sell to reach your fundraising goal?

CHANGEMAKERS

Mabel Ping-Hua Lee was just 15 years old when she led a march for women's voting rights in New York City in 1912. Even more impressive, Mabel was fighting for rights that she believed in but would be denied. Back then, Chinese people were largely banned from immigrating to the United States, and the few that did faced immense discrimination. Mabel, as a Chinese woman, wasn't allowed to become an American citizen and wouldn't be able to vote herself. Still, she fought for change for others.

RIPPLE EFFECT: an interview with
PEYTON KLEIN (she/her), ANTI-DISCRIMINATION ACTIVIST

Peyton Klein started the Global Minds Initiative at her high school in Pittsburgh, Pennsylvania, in 2016. Since then, Peyton's idea of an after-school club to foster intercultural friendships between English language learners and English-speaking students has grown into an international movement. Now, more than 3600 students in 25 schools around the world participate in the program.

How did you get the idea for the Global Minds Initiative?

When I was 15, I volunteered for Hillary Clinton's 2016 U.S. presidential campaign. I believed in the values of diversity and inclusion and the welcoming of newcomers, and I was upset by the rhetoric discriminating against immigrants and refugees. Sitting in class one day after the election, I realized I knew everyone's name except for the quiet girl sitting behind me who wore a hijab. In that moment I understood that while I believed in the values of diversity, inclusion and welcoming, I wasn't actually living by those values. So I went up to this girl and I learned that her name was Khwalah. We started chatting every morning. We talked about biology class and learning to drive. She told me about her experience leaving Syria and the racism she faced at school. I helped her with biology assignments and how to talk to her school counselor. Our friendship enriched both of our lives. It got me thinking: *How could we help other students to connect? How could we better support English language learners?* So I started the Global

Minds Initiative. In the beginning, the program was just 10 students in one classroom. Before long, we had 100 students filling up the hallways.

How have your experiences shaped your thinking about the power of youth to bring about social change?

Being for youth and by youth is totally key to Global Minds' success. There are a lot of organizations that engage youth but not in leadership positions. Global Minds is about intercultural education, global friendship and fostering inclusivity. But it's also about empowering young people to use their voices and agency for social change with the support of adult allies. One thing that's incredible about youth leadership is that young people are able to see the big picture. While adults are arguing about logistics, ownership and tedious details, young people take action. Youth mobilize very fast in ways that other generations couldn't because of our exposure and access to social media. And I'm excited by what that means for social change.

What advice do you have for young activists?

Listen. Ask questions. Learn before you do. *Then* do. To be an activist, you need a "just do it" mindset. If, after you've listened, you just start working — knowing that you will get something wrong — you're on the right track.

To learn how to start a Global Minds Initiative chapter at your school, go to www.globalminds.world.

BE A
CHANGEMAKER

You are an activist. And anyone can be! Change comes from the actions — big and small — of people with diverse talents and strengths.

You have the power to improve lives. Learning about the social and environmental injustices in your community and around the world can be overwhelming. But once you understand the challenges, you'll know where you want to focus your efforts to help.

Your contribution matters. Use your unique strengths and talents to make change.

2

EDUCATE

"I'm not sure I can afford college anymore," a classmate confessed. Our provincial government had just announced budget cuts that would result in teacher layoffs, increased class sizes and reduced financial support for post-secondary education. When I realized the impact these cuts would have on my classmates — and so many others, like my sister, who was starting university — I knew I had to do something.

But first, I needed to learn more: When would the budget cuts be approved? What had people done to fight education budget cuts in the past? What worked? Had anyone else started taking action? Through my research, I learned about Students Say No, a group of students fighting the policy changes. After reading their mission statement and agreeing with their goals, I signed up to work with the group.

Students Say No was organizing a one-day provincial walkout in protest. My sister and I worked with other interested students to organize speakers, raise awareness through social media, communicate with our school administrators, contact the media for coverage and circulate petitions. Overall, the walkout at my school was a huge success. More than 300 students participated and over 1000 people signed the "No Cuts to Schools" petition. Plus, we stood in solidarity with 100 000 students across the province. Most importantly, we were able to educate one another about the proposed government budget cuts that could affect our education.

THE WORLD AROUND YOU

The way you see the world is shaped by your family and friends, your culture and beliefs (both conscious and unconscious) — and your privilege. The advantages the groups you belong to have — or the challenges they face — will affect the ideas and perspectives you're exposed to and the experiences you have. And that, in turn, will shape what you think is right and wrong, fair and unfair.

If you're serious about activism, you'll need to spend some time thinking about why you believe the things you do. Sometimes we develop biases — both conscious and unconscious — about other groups. Have you ever been taught something about a group and later found out that it wasn't true? Or have you questioned the stereotypes used to justify discriminating against a marginalized group? Examine your own biases. Be open to learning about viewpoints and experiences that are very different from your own. Learning more about the world will help you to form your own opinions. And as your understanding of social justice issues grows, you'll be better able to focus your energies and identify the things you want to help change.

MARGINALIZED GROUPS:

Marginalized groups are those that have historically experienced discrimination and exclusion due to social, economic, educational and/or cultural differences. These can include factors such as race, gender identity, sexual orientation, age, ability, religion, immigration status, class and many others.

PRIVILEGE:

Privilege is the social power and advantages you are granted by society as a member of a particular group.

THINK LIKE AN
ACTIVIST

- Look at the world around you with an open mind.
- Question what you have been taught to believe: *Why do I think this way? Is it true? Is it fair?*
- Identify inequities you want to change.
- Stand up for people who are treated unfairly.
- Do what you think is right even when others disagree.

KNOWLEDGE IS
POWER
UNDERSTANDING THE ISSUE

The social justice issues we see in our communities and around the world don't just develop out of nowhere. They have long and complex histories. To understand how these injustices have built up over time, you have to do your research. For your activism to have an impact, it has to be rooted in facts. Remember, your friends who are experiencing the injustice aren't historical scholars and can't be expected to know everything about the issue. And respect that they may be sensitive about the issue and may not want to have to teach you about a painful topic. Seek out existing resources and educate yourself. By knowing as much as you can about an issue, you'll be able to advocate effectively and convince others to join the fight!

FACTS	OPINIONS
Facts are undeniably true.	Opinions are what people think about something. Sometimes they're based on facts. Sometimes they're not.
FACT: The sky is blue.	OPINION: Blue clothes are boring.

Of course, in the real world, social justice issues don't fit into a nice, neat box. Inequality and injustice come from a combination of racism, sexism, classism, ableism, homophobia, transphobia and other kinds of discrimination and hate. Their long tendrils intertwine with one another and can cause stress, depression, anger and anxiety. Worst of all, these injustices are deeply rooted in and perpetuated by legal, educational and other institutions. Not all groups of people have the same political and economic power — and sadly that means that not all groups receive equal treatment and opportunities. You'll encounter many examples of institutional inequalities in your activism journey. For example, in researching intergenerational poverty, you'll identify other injustices people might be facing, such as a lack of access to education.

CHANGEMAKERS

Everyone knows that Rosa Parks was the first Black woman to refuse to give up her seat on a bus in Montgomery, Alabama, to fight segregation, right? Wrong! Rosa Parks was not the first. Nine months earlier, 15-year-old Claudette Colvin was arrested and sent to adult jail. But because of her dark skin and natural hair, civil rights leaders didn't think Claudette was the best representative for the fight. (The prejudice that favors people with lighter skin over those with darker skin is called colorism and continues today.) Plus, they didn't believe a teen would be reliable. So Rosa Parks, who was older, fairer skinned and already respected in the Civil Rights Movement, was chosen to be the face of the struggle. Claudette kept fighting, though. She challenged the discriminatory law in court along with three other women — and their case would successfully overturn the bus segregation laws in Alabama.

WHERE TO FIND
GOOD INFORMATION
CHEAP

- Online news sites and apps with vetted, fact-based, fact-checked work, such as BBC Newsround and NPR
- Institutions and museums, such as the National Center for Civil and Human Rights, the American Civil Liberties Union and the Canadian Museum for Human Rights
- National archives, such as the U.S. National Archives
- Local historical societies, such as the Historical Society of Ottawa
- Recently published library books written by a trusted author

TIP:

Keep track of when and where you find key pieces of information. Then, if people question or challenge your information, you can cite the source to prove your facts. Use fact-checking sites like www.snopes.com to check info.

To guide your research and to gain a deeper understanding of all the factors contributing to a particular injustice, **ask yourself these important questions:**

- Why does this social justice issue exist?
- Is the injustice widespread in political or social institutions?
- Is the injustice perpetuated by the practices and habits of many?
- Have there been efforts to combat the injustice in the past? What has worked? What hasn't worked?
- What roadblocks did activists face in the past? Do the roadblocks still exist?

SEEING THE
BIG PICTURE

It takes a community of people to make change. Once you know the issue you want to focus on, reach out to others to expand your knowledge and to develop a network of like-minded friends and supporters (and get some of your questions answered). Many groups will already have campaigns and initiatives underway. If the group's mission statement and goals align with yours, you may even want to join and focus your efforts on their good work!

Even if the group's goals are different from yours, there may be ways for you to work together. Having relationships with larger, existing groups will offer you support and credibility and may encourage more people to join your movement. You can ask other groups to share information about your cause (and offer to do the same for them!). Other groups may also have connections to local media, government and changemakers in your area that they are open to sharing.

REACHING OUT TO OTHER GROUPS

Hi, **[organization's name]**,

My name is **[your name]** and I'm hoping to get more involved in **[your cause]**. **[Explain your journey into activism and why you want to get involved. This will give them a better sense of your passion and show them your commitment.]**

I am interested in your group and was wondering if you could tell me more about your current projects. I am hoping to **[tell them about your goals to help them see if you're a good fit for their team]**.

If you're accepting volunteers or can put me in contact with someone in the group, I'd greatly appreciate it.

Thank you for your time. I look forward to speaking more.

Sincerely,

[Your name]

EMAIL TEMPLATE

MISSION STATEMENTS

You can learn a lot about an organization and the work they do from their mission statement. Here's an example:

EcoClub Mission Statement: We will be working to minimize waste in our school. Our first goal is to reduce plastic water bottle use. We will accomplish this by educating students about the dangers of plastic and the reusable options they can use instead.

Ask yourself:

- Is the mission statement well thought out? Carefully crafted? Does it allow the organization to grow?
- Do I agree with the group's mission statement? Do their activities support it?

If you answer yes to the questions above, you'll know it's a group you might want to join or collaborate with. If your initiatives and goals are different, you can reach out to make connections but continue your own work independently.

RIPPLE EFFECT: an interview with
ANNALEE RAIN YELLOWHAMMER (she/her), WATER PROTECTOR

In 2016, when AnnaLee Rain Yellowhammer was 13 years old, she and 30 other youth members of the Standing Rock Sioux Tribe started a petition to raise awareness and prevent construction of the Dakota Access Pipeline (DAPL). Over 150 000 people signed the petition and thousands gathered at Standing Rock in protest, bringing international attention to their cause. AnnaLee and the other youth activists continue to fight to #ShutDownDAPL.

What was it like to start a movement?

I felt disbelief at the response to #NoDAPL — in a good way. I could never have imagined how many people would be interested in our message. And I could never have imagined the experiences I would have. Our group ReZpect Our Water did a relay run from Standing Rock to Washington, DC, to deliver the letter I wrote to the Army Corps of Engineers. My letter explained how if the pipeline broke, it would threaten not only our drinking water supply but the land we have called home for generations. The run was the first time I had ever traveled anywhere without my siblings, mother or grandmother. But we had good guidance, and the peers that I traveled with are my lifelong family.

Why did you think it was so important to educate people about the environmental and cultural impact of pipelines?

It was my grandmother who inspired me to get involved. I want to be the voice for my ancestors, my community and future generations. Mni wiconi — Water Is Life. Our water is very important to us. The waterways are a sacred way of life. If the pipeline broke, it would pollute our water and harm the people, land and animals and threaten our sacred burial grounds.

How do you keep motivated?

It gets tough. There are times when I've tried to quit or taken a step back. I know I have to love myself because everything comes from that. Then, I tell myself that there are brighter days ahead and to keep pushing forward.

What advice would you give young activists?

Keep going no matter what. Even if you don't believe in yourself, I believe in you.

CAN YOU KNOW **EVERYTHING?**

We all wish we knew everything — especially related to an injustice we feel passionately about. But the reality is that no one knows everything! Your education, in and outside of the classroom, has had its own biases. Some perspectives and historical truths have been omitted. Not to mention that it's impossible to know everything in a changing world. New ideas, initiatives, processes and resources are always developing. So you have to keep learning! Instead of seeing this as a roadblock to your activism career, embrace it as motivation to keep going. Don't be afraid to ask questions if you don't understand. Make sure the information you share is factual, unbiased and *current*. And be on the lookout for new ways of communicating information for maximum impact.

CHANGEMAKERS

In the 1980s, tens of thousands of Americans — mostly gay men — were dying of HIV/AIDS. The government was doing little to understand the disease and was not offering public health information. So in 1987, a group of gay artists and activists, Avram Finkelstein, Brian Howard, Oliver Johnston, Charles Kreloff, Chris Lione and Jorge Socarrás, started the Silence=Death Project. The artists designed a poster to motivate their community to organize politically and to protest the government's inaction. Silence=Death was written in large type on a black background. The only image was a pink triangle, a reference to the triangle the Nazis forced homosexuals to wear during the Holocaust. The artists joined with ACT UP (AIDS Coalition to Unleash Power) on the campaign, inspiring many to take political action to raise awareness about the crisis and the need for research on treatment. The Silence=Death image was reproduced on buttons, stickers and T-shirts and became the symbol of AIDS activism around the world.

BE A
CHANGEMAKER

You have your own informed opinions. Learning about your community, your country and the big wide world, along with your own biases, gives you a deeper understanding of the issues.

You can share what you learn to educate others. When you've researched all aspects of an injustice — its history as well as current challenges and efforts to address it — you can confidently share unbiased, factual information with others.

You will continue to learn about issues. To make change and grow your movement, you have to continue to learn new information and develop skills to support your cause.

3

ACT

One summer day, my friends and I met to go biking on a favorite local trail. When we arrived, the trail was completely flooded. Broken tree branches were strewn all over and murky water covered the path. Earlier in the month, some severe storms had hit our area, flooding the waterfront. As I stood there with my disappointed friends, I realized that my environmental activism wasn't just about fighting for our future. There was work to be done now!

I'd heard that other cities had declared a state of climate emergency and thought, *Why not us?* If the city government acknowledged the negative impact climate change was already having in the area, then it would have to commit to addressing the causes and effects. I decided to lead the charge to have my city declare a climate emergency. I wrote up a plan of action and shared it with my school eco team, my friends, my family and other local activists for their input. Then we got to work.

To show the city that its residents cared about this initiative, I collected around 150 signatures on a petition. Some of my classmates wrote letters supporting the proposal. Then, I applied to be an official delegate at a municipal council meeting. With the guidance and support of many and the eco team cheering me on, I presented to the municipal council. At first, I was intimidated by the mayor and city councillors, but when I started speaking, my confidence returned. I believed passionately in the importance of the declaration. I'd rehearsed my speech many times and I knew exactly what I wanted to say. And the proposal to declare an official climate emergency in my city was passed.

Now, a number of initiatives are underway. To start, a study of the waterfront led to proposals on how to make the waterfront accessible regardless of weather conditions. The city decided to build an elevated walkway! The city is also investing in a tree-planting program, expanding our pollinator habitats and using new energy-saving heating, ventilation and air-conditioning units in city-run spaces! Although my city still has a long way to go, this was a huge step in the right direction.

BE THE
CHANGE

Fighting to bring about change you believe in can be overwhelming. When you're ready to take action to support a cause that's important to you, it's natural to be unsure of where to start. So, take it slow. First, reflect on *why* you have to act for your cause now. Then, think about what you learned in your research and draft a plan that lays out your vision and goals. Ask yourself questions like *What do I want to accomplish? Who am I trying to reach? What's the best way to do that?* There are different ways to meet your goals. Writing to politicians, making a donation and marching in the streets are all examples of taking action. Organizing rallies, speaking at events and creating social media campaigns are direct, accessible ways to share clear, credible information to raise awareness and draw people to your cause.

HOW TO ...
RAISE AWARENESS

To raise awareness about your cause, you can go big: organizing a protest, a walkout or a rally. Or you can go small: starting a conversation, forming a club or inviting people to a seminar. Whether your initiative is big or small, it will accomplish many of the same goals, such as

- building awareness
- recruiting and mobilizing people
- showing there is support for your initiative
- giving people a safe place to gather
- attracting attention to your cause

CHANGEMAKERS

In Saudi Arabia, where Manal al-Sharif was born in 1979, it was illegal for women to drive. In 2011, the computer scientist and women's rights activist launched a movement, Women2Drive, campaigning for women's right to drive. She posted a video of herself driving on social media to promote the campaign. When authorities saw the post, al-Sharif was arrested and jailed for nine days. But the movement she started led to the law being repealed in 2018.

WHAT ACTION IS **RIGHT** FOR YOUR CAUSE?

Having trouble deciding what action to take? This flowchart will help. Use these general actions as a springboard for developing your own amazing ideas!

START HERE

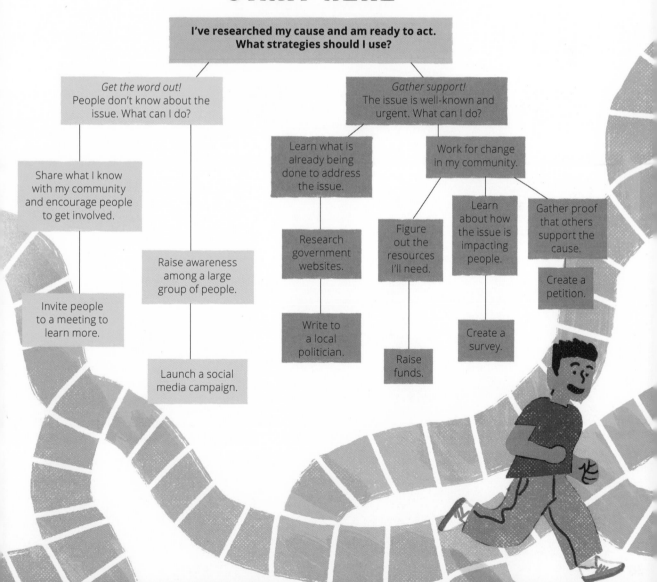

I've researched my cause and am ready to act. What strategies should I use?

Get the word out! People don't know about the issue. What can I do?

- Share what I know with my community and encourage people to get involved.
  - Invite people to a meeting to learn more.
- Raise awareness among a large group of people.
  - Launch a social media campaign.

Gather support! The issue is well-known and urgent. What can I do?

- Learn what is already being done to address the issue.
  - Research government websites.
    - Write to a local politician.
- Work for change in my community.
  - Figure out the resources I'll need.
    - Raise funds.
  - Learn about how the issue is impacting people.
    - Create a survey.
  - Gather proof that others support the cause.
    - Create a petition.

SPEAK UP

Whether you're talking to hundreds of people at a protest or to a handful of classmates, **your speech needs to**

- grab your audience's attention
- convince people to support your cause
- send out an "ask." Be clear about what you want them to be thinking about when your speech is over — and what actions they can take.

Dealing with Nerves

Whenever I'm talking in front of a crowd or answering an important phone call, I get butterflies in my stomach. I feel like I'm on a roller coaster that's about to drop! I try to remind myself that it's okay to be nervous. Even if I do make a small mistake, it's nothing anyone will really notice or care about in the long run. Still, when you've been anticipating a moment for so long, or when a lot of people are paying attention to you, it's normal to get a little worried about it. I've slowly learned that my nerves mostly come from excitement. Now, I try to embrace the nerves and remind myself that this enthusiasm will make for a more passionate conversation!

Connecting with Your Audience

Speaking with emotion helps you connect with your audience. Your enthusiasm and expression can make a speech more vivid and memorable than reading an article or seeing an ad. Try these tips:

- Color-code words in your speech to remind you to either take a dramatic pause or say a word with *lots* of expression.
- Memorize the key passages of your speech. This way, you can make eye contact with the audience when you're delivering the main idea or final statement — for maximum emotional impact. And when you know the important messages you want to get across, you'll deliver them with more confidence.

Keeping the Conversation Going

Whatever the size of the group, and whether I'm speaking in person or to the media, I ask the audience if they have any questions. (If I can't answer them at the time, I let people know how to contact me.) I try to prepare, but it's impossible to know everything about a topic. Sometimes I just don't know the answer. So here's what I do!

WHEN YOU DON'T KNOW
WHAT TO SAY

1. **Say that you're not sure.** Let the person know that while you are educated on the topic, you still have much to learn!

    Example: "Sorry, I know a bit about the subject but not enough to answer your question in detail."

2. **Give them a way to get their question answered.** Suggest next steps and resources they can access.

    Example: "Someone at this nonprofit organization would know more about this topic and be able to answer your question."

3. **Find out the answer to the question.** Do your research and draft a response based on your new knowledge. Practice answering the question — it may come up again! Your commitment to educating yourself may inspire others, too. Reading a book, looking through news articles or asking a reliable source are all ways to prepare yourself if this question is ever asked again!

CHANGEMAKERS

When Ed Roberts was 14, he got polio and was paralyzed in most of his lower body. But that didn't stop him from pursuing his dreams. He was accepted at the prestigious University of California, Berkeley, in 1962 — the first student there ever to use a wheelchair. Then, he convinced the university to accept more students with disabilities. Ed and other students with disabilities formed a group called the Rolling Quads. They pressured the university to add ramps and curb cuts to make the classrooms and dorm buildings more accessible and provide disability services, such as transportation and wheelchair repair. Ed and the other Rolling Quads started a movement that increased our understanding of disability rights and led to more accessible spaces that we see today.

GET POLITICAL

Use your age to your advantage! Many politicians are excited to hear from youth. The government is in charge of so many things, including what you study at school, how safe your food is, who can be a citizen and a lot of other issues that affect you every day. Advocating for your cause to make change to government legislation can have a large and long-term impact.

LEVELS OF GOVERNMENT

Local: in charge of issues of daily life in your community (e.g., road safety, bike lanes)

Provincial or state: responsible for laws and policies for people in your province or state (e.g., school curricula, provincial and state parks)

Federal: in charge of developing laws and decisions that affect the whole country (e.g., immigration, banking)

International: organizations of different countries that form alliances to pass laws and policies on global issues (e.g., climate change, refugee crisis)

Your first step is ensuring you're directing your activism toward the correct level of government and the right politician — the one who's in power, in charge of this issue and able to make change. After I witnessed the flooding on my city's waterfront, I researched and found out this was my local government's responsibility. I learned about the municipal council for my city on the local government website and created a list of the local officials I could contact.

When approaching government, make a focused request. The more specific your request is, the more likely a politician will respond to you. Show them that you've done your research and are committed to your cause. Before presenting to the council, I looked into the municipality's current environmental policies and researched neighboring municipalities to learn about new initiatives my city could adopt.

Then, I put my knowledge and passion on paper. I used the letter template on the next page for this initiative — and many others since.

[Your name]
[Your address]
[Any important contact information you would like to share, such as your phone number or email]
[Date]

[Full name of the person you're addressing]
[Their title]
[Area of government]
[Their address]

Dear **[Title or Name]**,

TIP:
The proper way to address government officials varies depending on the level of government. Check online to make sure you address your letter correctly.

Paragraph 1:
Start with an attention-grabbing opening sentence.
    Example: "The sky is falling!! The sky is falling!!" Following a severe tornado, the
    citizens of St. Louis, Missouri, are now facing homelessness due to collapsed shelters.
Introduce yourself.
Summarize your cause (answer the *who, what, where* and *how* in two sentences or less).
What would you like the government to do? Make this a very brief, factual statement.

Paragraph 2:
Explain why this is important to you personally and how it affects the politician. Why should they care? Why does this matter?

Paragraph 3:
Discuss the government's next steps in more depth. What exactly can they do and how? Explain the cause in more detail. Using statistics, explain why this affects your community.

Paragraph 4:
Conclude by summarizing the purpose of the letter. Encourage the politician to take action on your issue. Thank the politician for their time.

Sincerely,

[Signature]
[Your name]

GATHERING
SUPPORT

Sometimes to advocate effectively, you need to show that you're not acting alone. A petition is a great way to demonstrate that others support your cause. Petitions can also help to raise awareness. The kind of petition you choose will depend on your cause and goals.

TIP:
Before creating an online petition, or sharing an existing one with your followers, research the site you're using and go through the signing process yourself to make sure the site is legitimate and doesn't require the people who sign to donate.

Sharing online petitions can reach a lot of people and make collecting many signatures extremely easy. In asking people to sign, you raise awareness and educate others about your cause.

Canvassing a petition is a great way to raise awareness about your cause in your community. Because you're approaching people directly to sign, you'll get a better sense of the range of opinions on the issue and how to focus your communications. Best of all, in talking with people about why they should sign, you may gain support for your cause or find others who want to volunteer. Here's an example: Create a petition for your school to have a silent dance to be more inclusive of neurodiverse students. After collecting ideas, signatures and support, take it to the principal to report your findings!

Petitioning the government is a great way to work for sustainable change — and to give your cause credibility. To create a petition the government will recognize, you need to follow a very specific set of rules so that every signature counts. At one protest, I passed around a petition and asked everyone to sign. One signatory didn't fill out his address, and the people signing after him assumed they didn't have to, either. When I got the petition back, I saw that I wasn't able to include these signatures because they didn't follow every rule! Research the rules for your area and the level of government you're petitioning. Some government petitions require certain wording, so look through a few sample petitions first.

GATHERING
INFORMATION

Surveys are an easy way to collect data from a group of people. You can use them in a school, a community, a neighborhood or a club!

The survey results will give you a deeper understanding of people's feelings about a topic — often contradicting your assumptions — and can help direct your actions.

You can use surveys for something as simple as asking your eco team, *What is the best day to meet?*, or as complex as helping a community calculate their accumulated carbon footprint. If you're surveying a large, diverse group, make sure to get responses from a wide range of people.

Make the survey anonymous. Especially if the survey is about topics some people may be ashamed or anxious about, let survey takers know their answers are confidential so they are comfortable answering truthfully.

HOW TO ...
CREATE A SURVEY

- Research online survey tools. If you decide to use existing survey software, make sure it's from an established, credible site. Or use what you've learned to create your own survey on paper.
- Make sure your questions are not biased. By keeping your questions neutral, you will get more accurate results.

BIASED	NEUTRAL
How has the federal government's immigration policy disappointed you?	On a scale of 1–10, where 10 is extremely satisfied and 1 is not at all satisfied, how satisfied are you with the federal government's immigration policy?

MONEY TALKS

Fundraising is an important tool for activists. In fact, sometimes fundraising *is* the activism! Fundraising can be:

- raising money or collecting goods to donate directly to people
- raising funds to cover the costs of some of your initiatives

Either type of fundraising campaign requires careful planning and management. Before you begin, find a trusted adult to act as an advisor for the project. Ask yourself: *What resources do we need? Are there free resources we can access?* Start by creating a budget projecting how much money you'll need and how it will be used. Here are some other questions to ask:

- What's the minimum amount of money needed to accomplish this initiative? If we raise more, what will we use it for?
- What expenses will we have for our fundraising campaign?
- What will we do with the money we raise? (Ideas: deposit it in a bank account; keep it in a cash box; ask a nonprofit to manage the funds.)

HOT DOGS $2
VEG DOGS $2
BURGERS $

FUNDRAISING MADE EASY

- To encourage others to donate, consider offering an incentive. Hold a raffle or auction, organize a car wash, plan a barbecue, use your own skills and strengths! For example, a group of students in Ontario sold baked goods to raise bail funds for Black Lives Matter (BLM) protesters.
- If you can't offer an incentive, don't worry. Just remind people why you're raising money and what it'll be used for — and ask them to give what they can.
- If you're considering an online fundraising platform, do your research. Learn about what services they offer and what obligations you have. Does the platform take a percent of the funds raised? Which interface best suits your needs?
- Store cash donations in a lockbox and keep a running list of how much you've raised, along with donor names for thank-you cards.
- Track your actual expenses throughout the campaign to make sure you're not overspending. You want the money you raise to go to your cause.
- Remember, even if someone is supportive of your cause, they may not be able to donate … and that's okay! Suggest other ways they can help out. Businesses in your community may be able to offer support, too. Donations of food, graphic design services, craft supplies or space for meetings all help your campaign.

RIPPLE EFFECT: an interview with
RAE PAUL (they/them), 2SLGBTQIA+ ACTIVIST

Rae Paul, a social worker, works at the Youth Project in Halifax, Nova Scotia. As the BIPOC community engagement coordinator, they connect with, support and create affirming spaces for 2SLGBTQIA+ youth of color. But their activism started a decade earlier in high school.

Why did you get involved in activism?

In grade 9, I was having a hard time coming to terms with my queerness. There was no positive representation of queer butches of color for me, especially in a faith community. I felt that there wasn't a place for queerness in my life as I knew it. In grade 10, I approached the chaplain at my school. He was the first adult I came out to who affirmed my humanity. His response was "You're fine. It's okay to be queer." And it turned into a bigger conversation about the need for space for queer students to foster community belonging at our school. Our school board has a history of stonewalling queer activism, but there was an anti-bullying law being passed that protected students' right to name a club a Gay-Straight Alliance (GSA). So I wanted to start a GSA at my school. The chaplain said that I could do that but calling it a GSA would cause a lot of backlash with the administration. He asked, "So what could we do that would have the greatest impact?" We came up with the idea of calling it Alliance for Compassion. How can you argue with compassion? We were doing a lot of local social justice initiatives. And I was able to create a space for myself where I could do things that are in line with my values while being supported by adults and by my peers.

How do you create safe spaces for youth activism?

For me, anytime I've worked with youth and had great experiences, it was because we had a relationship of trust. A relationship of trust comes from really listening. Youth are told all the time what to do, what to wear, how to act. When someone says "What do you think?" and listens and doesn't give advice and doesn't shut them down, it makes space for youth to say "I have this idea." It makes space for creativity. In activism, you cannot be everything and you cannot be everywhere. It shouldn't be just you. If it's just you, and you're only doing stuff for yourself, it won't be sustainable or joyful. To create a braver space, you have to be able to say "I see you and I'm going to have your back. I know we're committed to the same goals. Even when you mess up, I'm going to have your back."

What is your advice for young activists?

Your heart is good. There is nothing wrong with you. Even when people say that you're not doing what you're supposed to be doing and push back against your activism, know you are still good. Even if you fail, you're still good. There's this idea that you need to do everything perfectly and know everything, and it fosters shame where love can reside. No one knows everything. Failure is a sweet teacher — sometimes even more than success. The sooner we learn this as youth and make space for failure, the better off we'll be. If we allow failure to be a teacher, we can learn so much more about how we can create change.

BE A
CHANGEMAKER

You understand there are many ways to take action.
You're aware of the wide range of strategies and campaigns
that activists use to work toward social change.

You choose your actions — and words — carefully.
You consider your issue and your goals before deciding on
a strategy.

You collaborate to meet your goals. You realize that only
through continued learning and collaborating with others
will you meet your goals.

4

CONNECT

You never know the impact your message is going to have. Once, after giving an activism workshop to a group of high school students, I was approached by a girl a few years younger than me. She began asking me how I got involved in activism. I was excited to share my experiences and offer suggestions. I loved her enthusiasm and we had an instant connection. After a few minutes, our conversation shifted to our career goals and I told her how I wanted to pursue computer science. She confessed that she didn't know much about it and, eager to share, I described how I'd developed my interests in coding and math. We talked about the lack of women in the field and why it was so important to have people with diverse perspectives and experiences working on projects in the industry.

Throughout our conversation, I was moved by how genuinely interested the young girl was in what I had to say. Later, she found my email and wrote to tell me that she had enrolled in a coding camp. I was thrilled by her news — and grateful that my passion for getting more girls into STEM had an impact.

SPREADING THE WORD

Words are powerful. The messaging you use conveys everything about your issue and campaign — and needs to answer these key questions:

- Who are you or who is your group?
- What is the issue or problem?
- Why should people care?
- What must we do to solve it?

CALLS TO ACTION

Practice these powerful statements in the mirror before a speech or workshop. It will help you to speak confidently and with emotion.

HOW MUCH LONGER WILL YOU ALLOW THIS TO HAPPEN?

ARE YOU WILLING TO MAKE A DIFFERENCE?

THE TIME FOR US TO ACT IS NOW.

MAKING IT
PERSONAL

We've all encountered people who present an idealized version of their life on social media. Everything just seems too perfect, and we don't trust that it's an authentic reflection of them. By being truthful, honest and open about your struggles as an activist, people will see your genuine passion for your cause.

Whether you're speaking to a crowd or having a one-on-one conversation, sharing personal stories is an excellent way to make an emotional connection. *When did you discover how urgent your issue was? Have you experienced or witnessed the injustice you're fighting?* Sharing a personal anecdote will convey why this cause is so important to you. More importantly, your story will humanize the issue and compel people to pause and reflect on their *own* actions.

GROWING YOUR
SQUAD

Now that you've got others interested in the movement, you need to convince them to take action! But first you need to earn their trust. Remember, everyone has their own interests and concerns. Do your research and ask your audience questions so you know their priorities. Tailor your message to make it clear that your cause speaks to their concerns. For example, when giving an advocacy workshop to a women's group, I suggested women's shelters where they could volunteer because I knew they'd be interested in that work.

HOW TO ...
PERSUADE OTHERS TO TAKE ACTION

- Share stories of strategic actions that brought change.
- Provide resources on how to get involved.
- Appeal to logic. Refer to statistics and facts when appropriate.
- Use and cite credible sources, and give the information in concise, confident statements.
- Convey the urgent need for action.
- Provide realistic, specific steps to take rather than only making broad statements like "take action."

CHANGEMAKERS

In 2008, Barack Obama's campaign slogan "Yes We Can" took him all the way to the White House. But he wasn't the first to use this hopeful message. Way back in 1962, activist Dolores Huerta coined a similar phrase in Spanish: "Sí, se puede," which translates to "Yes, it can be done!" or "Yes, you can." "Sí, se puede" was the rallying cry for the United Farm Workers of America, who fought for fair wages and safe working conditions for Latinx farmworkers. And President Obama was clearly a fan of Huerta's — in 2012, he awarded her the Presidential Medal of Freedom.

THE
POWER
OF
ARTIVISM

By being creative and using your talents and gifts, you can have fun, stand out and reach a new audience. For Pride month, a member of our Alliance for Compassion club custom-made personalized Pride bracelets for the different flags of the community that represent gay, lesbian, bisexual, asexual, pansexual, intersex, trans and genderqueer identities. My friend Sophia Mathur, a dancer, held Earth Dances, a showcase for talented dancers in her community, to fundraise for climate action. How will you use your talent for your cause?

ARTIVIST:
Someone who raises awareness and works to make social change through the creation of art.

RIPPLE EFFECT: an interview with
MANSOOR HUSSAINI (he/him), PEACE AND EDUCATION ACTIVIST

For Mansoor Hussaini's whole life, his home country of Afghanistan has been at war. Since he was born in 1999, the Taliban, an Islamic fundamentalist group, has been fighting for power. Mansoor's family is at risk because they are Hazara, an ethnic group that the Taliban views as an enemy because of their Shi'a faith. At 13, Mansoor became involved with the Afghan Peace Volunteers (APV) and opened the Zaryab School for street kids. When the Taliban seized control in 2021, Mansoor was forced to flee.

How did you get involved and what did you do with the Afghan Peace Volunteers?
When I was in grade 10, I started teaching English at the "Street Kids School" run by the Afghan Peace Volunteers (APV). The APV was made up of Afghans of different ethnicities and religious sects. I was glad to find other youth and international activists who wanted to build peace. I realized I'd found my place. We distributed duvets and food to poor families, organized multiethnic youth conferences, taught conflict resolution, planted trees and planned solar energy projects. We even had a mock funeral for weapons in front of the Independent Human Rights Commission in Kabul. For APV's #Enough! Campaign, we got citizens from 56 countries to sign our petition saying no to war. I made videos, designed T-shirts and a bracelet, and spoke to classes.

Why did you want to teach street kids?
As a former street kid, I understood that these kids had to earn money for themselves and their families by selling cigarettes and chewing gum, washing cars and polishing shoes. The APV school was only open on Fridays, so a friend and I opened our own center to give kids a chance to study more. We taught classes early in the morning before kids had to work. Some older siblings started coming to our classes, too.

You made educating girls your priority. Why?
I saw how hard it was to be a girl in Afghanistan. Girls of all ethnicities had few opportunities to attend school beyond high school. Families that could afford it sent their sons to university, while girls were expected to marry and have children. But our girl students were thirsty for education. Many traveled long distances to school and did chores before class. They wanted the same chance as boys. So I started teaching free university preparation classes, and soon most of our students were girls.

Why did you continue running a school for girls when it was so dangerous?
Schools, hospitals and mosques were being bombed by Islamic State extremists. People were being killed every day. If I stopped, that still wouldn't stop. Education gives people a light. I stayed positive and was able to help more than 100 girls get accepted to universities.

What advice do you have for young activists?
Just because you're young doesn't mean your efforts aren't important. I learned from street kids that it's not about age. You don't have to be a grown-up to help your family, to do things. I experienced the same things. It's only about how brave you are. Age is just a number.

ACTIONS SPEAK LOUDER THAN **WORDS**

When fighting for a cause, you can't be all talk and no action. You need to be a conscious activist, taking small, consistent actions in your own life to support your cause. You may not be able to solve world hunger after school, but you can volunteer at a local food bank. I love thrifting with my friends. It's a great way to develop a unique style, save tons of clothes from the landfill ... and shop! Whenever someone compliments my outfit, I tell them it was thrifted — and we have an amazing conversation about sustainability and environmental activism!

CONSCIOUS ACTIVISM:

Activism by doing, by how you live your life, by what you consume — where you shop, what you eat, what you wear and other everyday choices.

CONSCIOUS ACTIVISM IS IN STYLE

Before you buy new clothes:

- Try shopping in your closet. Rediscover what you've forgotten.
- Set up a clothes swap with friends.
- DIY it! Get creative and restyle, cut, sew or repurpose what you have.
- Go thrifting for some new-to-you fashions.

Then, spread the word on sustainable style!

FINDING YOUR PEOPLE

As your activism grows, you may come up with initiatives that are too big for you or your friends to undertake on your own. To succeed, you might need to collaborate with other organizations. Always take the time to research the group to make sure their goals and values align with yours. Ask the following questions:

- How do they use the money they fundraise?
- Is their team diverse?
- How would your group benefit from this relationship?
- How would their group benefit from this relationship?
- What are the group's future goals?
- Are they aligned with your goals?
- Are they willing to collaborate with you?
- Are you willing to collaborate with them?

TIP:

Use this acronym to make sure you are collaborating with a **GOOD** group.

Goals are similar
Organized well
Open to others
Doesn't oppose your beliefs or ethics

STRONGER TOGETHER

Whether you're launching an initiative on your own or working with a large organization, you'll need the skills and support of others to succeed. Tap into your network to find people who can offer advice, expertise and volunteer power. Create a list of everyone you know, or know of, who can help your initiative in some way. You'll be surprised by how wide your network is. Include people of various ages and from different parts of your life: teachers, friends, family, fellow volunteers in another group, community members, local politicians and more. Don't worry if you don't know them well. Just telling them about your initiative may inspire them to get involved or introduce you to others who will!

As your movement grows, so can your network. By putting up an ad online, spreading the news through word of mouth and using your creativity to spark a buzz, you can continue drawing others to your cause.

HOW TO ... NETWORK

Begin by politely introducing yourself and reminding the person of your connection to each other. "Hi! My name is Charlene. We were in the same book club a few years ago. How are you?"

Chat with them for a bit and see how they're doing. The most important goal here is to create a stronger personal and professional connection with the other person. Next, tell them about your movement and ask if they would like to get involved!

"So, this weekend I'm having my first team meeting with this group I'm starting for _____ . Would you like to come? We'd love to have you! I can give you my email address if you want more info."

Be prepared to answer any questions they may have.

CHANGEMAKERS

When Drago Renteria, a trans man, transitioned in the late 1990s, he faced a great deal of homophobia and transphobia. Drago tried to find support, but he is deaf and there weren't many resources accessible to him. So he created them. Drago founded the first national resource center for the Deaf queer community in 1995, launched National Deaf LGBTQ Awareness Week in 2018 and much more. For more than three decades, he has been fighting to make sure that Deaf 2SLGBTQIA+ youth grow up feeling proud, empowered and knowing they are not alone. As Drago says, "If we do not act, we cannot create change."

MEDIA SMARTS

News outlets, social media accounts and podcasts can help you find an entirely new group of people and expand your reach. Pitching the media — getting in contact with the people who can amplify your message — is not easy. Neither is convincing them that your issue or movement is newsworthy. Use these strategies to build a connection and get them interested in your movement:

1. **Create a spreadsheet of journalists and their contact information.** Start locally, with your hometown newspaper, and slowly progress to bigger media platforms. This requires tons of research and time, but it's worth it. When you have a long list of contacts, draft a sample email and start sending it out to your list. Remember to update the name and any other details in the message before sending it. You're more likely to get a response when the email doesn't feel generic. If you can, try to speak to the reporter on the phone to build a connection.

2. **Share an intriguing and timely story about your movement to hook their interest.** Rather than describing your initiative, explain the *why* of your cause and its urgency in a dramatic way. Media will be more likely to follow up with you if you have a specific story that will hook their audience. For example, "160 million people are affected by natural disasters annually — here's how two elementary school students are helping" will interest more people than "Come to this fundraiser for natural disaster relief!"

3. **If you have an announcement about an event or initiative, you might want to create a media advisory or press release for news agencies.** A press release is an official statement sent to media. It should give journalists background information about your movement as well as details about a specific timely initiative.

Passion2Paint colors their city to raise $500 for classroom supplies

[City, Province/State] After discovering the Park District School Board didn't have money to buy art supplies, 31 grade 6 students have planned an art show titled "Passion2Paint" to support their class.

The students of Elm Public School were extremely upset when they heard they would no longer be able to paint in class. They didn't want their art studies to suffer because of the funding cuts.

Their teacher, Piper Pepper, commented, "These students are so passionate about art that the second I broke the bad news, they brainstormed ways to get more funding for art supplies. When one student mentioned creating their own art gallery in the school hallways, the whole class got on board to make the project soar."

Friends, family and community members are invited to attend the "Winter Wonderland"-themed original art show, which the students have been planning for a month.

The students hope to raise $500 for art supplies by charging a $5 entry fee. They hope to continue this project by helping other schools in their board raise money for their creative arts and drama classes.

To donate to their cause, or buy a ticket to the show, head to the Passion2Paint website!

Date: [Insert date]
Time: [Insert time]
Location: [Insert location]
Notes for Media:
[Where the media can find you if they attend the event]
Contact Information:
[Name of contact person, title, organization and phone number]

ACING THE INTERVIEW

Once you have successfully connected with the media, they may ask to interview you! This can be nerve-racking, but careful preparation always helps me feel more confident. Have your main points ready so you can communicate your movement's core message clearly and compellingly.

Think about the "image" you want to portray. What's the best strategy to encourage others to get involved? Do you want the audience to view you as knowledgeable, passionate, innovative or something else?

Try drafting sample responses to questions journalists may ask. Make sure your answers are concise and accurate. Always be prepared for these frequently asked questions:

Tell me about yourself.
What is your movement about?
How did you get involved?
What do you do?

Before an interview, think about what information you should keep private and what is okay to share. You will not have control over what gets included in the news story, so it's important to be careful what you say!

PROTECT THE PERSONAL

Remember to keep private information private. When you're being interviewed, don't share:

- your address
- your online alias
- stories you don't have permission to share

PLAYING IT SAFE ON
SOCIAL MEDIA

Social media is an easy, cost-efficient way to connect with a wide audience. And with the help of shares or reposts, your message can go viral — and bring new attention to your cause and campaign. That's why it's important to treat social media campaigns with respect. Remember, everything you say online leaves a digital footprint.

A great way to share clear and credible information is by creating graphics. Colorful, bold visuals can educate others and build awareness. Best of all, they are easily shared!

Social media can be a powerful tool for change. After TikTok launched around the world in 2017, it quickly became a digital gathering space for marginalized youth from diverse communities. Muslim, Deaf and trans activists used digital spaces to share their stories. By the early 2020s, Indigenous creators — known as NDN TikTokers — had embraced the platform and were having a big impact. Some young activists focused on educating their followers on topics such as Indigenous languages, history, culture and injustices, such as the residential school system and Missing and Murdered Indigenous Women and Girls. Others used the platform to call out racism or call for the return of stolen land. But one of the most exciting things about social media platforms is the way they make it easier for people from marginalized communities to connect online. Many NDN creators continue to post for other Indigenous Peoples. They're celebrating Indigenous life — not explaining or defending it, but being seen and being heard.

Of course, there are many online platforms you can use. Since many social media platforms have age requirements for users, talk to a trusted adult before joining. And remember to carefully think through every word, picture and comment you post to make sure it's clear and accurate. Look out for advertising and fake news disguised as personal posts. Before sharing, do some research to make sure the facts are correct.

BEFORE POSTING ON SOCIAL MEDIA, ASK YOURSELF:

- Is this information safe to share?
- Would I tell a stranger this?
- Are my points factual and accurate?
- What is my goal in sharing this?
- Will sharing this have a positive, negative or neutral impact?
- What emotions am I feeling as I post?
- Do I need to take a step back and return to this when I'm calmer and more prepared?
- Am I the right person to share this or speak on this?

Do you love the outdoors, making new friends and saving the planet? Join the Eco-Team in cleaning up Birch Lane Nature Trail!

Saturday, April 21, 10 a.m.

Meet in front of the library.
Dress for the weather and bring gloves.

Email ecoteam@greencity.com for more info.

BE A
CHANGEMAKER

You understand that connection is what inspires us to act.
You speak and act authentically to share your passion for your cause.

You work with other groups effectively. You understand the value of coordinating efforts for your cause.

You use media to promote your cause. You explore different media tactics to get your message out.

5

SUPPORT

After George Floyd, a victim of police brutality, was killed in 2020, I watched in awe as the Black Lives Matter movement inspired millions of protesters around the world to fight against anti-Black racism. Police brutality and anti-Black racism are realities in my community. Although I'll never be able to fully relate and speak to the experiences of my Black peers, I wanted to support the movement in any way I could. But first, I knew I needed to learn more about the issue. I attended seminars hosted by my school's Black history group. I accessed resources from Black activists and organizations. And most importantly, I listened to my Black peers.

My friend and classmate, Nathaniel Luces, a Black activist, really helped me to understand the issues — and my own unconscious bias — better. (Read more about Nathaniel's activism journey on page 90.)

Both Nathaniel and I joined the Break the Chains Pickering committee and got to work planning a peaceful protest. Yet, often I — not Nathaniel — would be asked for an interview or featured in a photo in a newspaper article about the protest. I realized that my role in supporting the cause was not just about what I did. It was about what I didn't do. I stepped back because Black committee members — those who were directly affected by the injustice — should lead and speak for the movement.

In the end, our protest was a huge success! More than 300 Pickering residents attended the event, and we gathered more than 600 signatures in support of updating Ontario school curriculum on Black Canadian history, as well as reforming policing systems in our province. More importantly, Black community members were able to speak directly to their neighbors and politicians about their lived experiences and offer ideas on how to move toward a better future.

CHECK YOUR
PRIVILEGE

Sometimes, we can feel defensive when we're told we have privilege — the social power one is granted by our society as a member of a particular group. Although we may be aware of some ways in which we're disadvantaged, the reality is we often don't realize the areas in which we may be privileged. Having privilege does not mean your life is easy. It just means certain aspects of your identity are not making your life more difficult. Take the time to reflect on the privilege you have and how you could use that privilege to better society.

ALTERNATIVE LIFE

Some things that you may take for granted are daily struggles in the lives of others. How would your life change if you had to deal with these challenges?

- Your community doesn't have clean, safe water. You have to use bottled water for drinking, cooking and even baths.
- You're not allowed to go to school in your country.
- After learning about your disability, people often speak to you in a degrading "baby" voice.
- Since your mom got laid off, your family struggles to afford groceries.
- When you watch movies or shows, you rarely see those who look like you. If you do, they're usually unflattering stereotypes.
- Your parents work at night, so you have to take care of your younger siblings and can't participate in after-school clubs and sports.
- You were fired for refusing to remove your religious headwear at work.
- In school, you never learn about your own culture and heritage.

EQUALITY vs. EQUITY

The world is filled with injustices, so we need to distribute our resources to ensure everyone has access to what they need. This is the key difference between equity and equality: Equality means everyone gets the same as everyone else. Equity means everyone gets what is just.

Imagine we're donating warm blankets to families during the winter. If we follow the terms of equality, which state everyone gets the same resources, we give every family one blanket, whether they need it or not. But if we follow the rules of equity, we provide the warm blankets to the families who are unhoused or living without heat and need the blankets the most. This way, everyone can stay warm in the cold.

CHANGEMAKERS

In the summer of 1964, more than 700 mostly white college students from across the U.S. traveled to Mississippi to participate in the Mississippi Summer Project. The students volunteered to help register African Americans to vote and also assisted in fighting intimidation and discrimination at the polls. They faced strong resistance from the Ku Klux Klan and some local sheriffs and state police. Volunteers were beaten and jailed. Three young civil rights workers, James Chaney, Andrew Goodman and Michael Schwerner, were murdered by the Ku Klux Klan. Still, the staff and student allies continued on their mission, raising awareness about the need for federal voting rights legislation, which led to the Voting Rights Act of 1965.

MORE THAN
GOOD INTENTIONS

You need more than good intentions to be a good ally. By supporting marginalized groups, you can use your privilege and power to bring attention to an issue and amplify the voices of those who are affected.

When I'm feeling down because of a comment made toward me or an incident in the news, I appreciate that my friends take the time to try and understand my perspective. Even if they'll never fully grasp the way I'm feeling, they're showing that they're willing to help in the fight against these injustices. In the same way, I want to advocate for others — I know how important it is to have a community of supporters!

ALLYSHIP:

Allyship means helping or supporting other people who are part of a group that is treated badly or unfairly, even if you are not a member of that group. It requires active listening, unlearning biases, building relationships and taking action.

PASSING ON THE MIC

Supporting a movement means listening and learning — not talking about what a good ally you are! Rather than just pushing your own ideas, hear what people who are directly affected have to say, support their proposals and volunteer to help with actions as directed.

Remember, you may not be the best person to answer a question or make a decision. If you're approached to speak on an issue that does not personally affect you, pass the opportunity to someone who has firsthand experience and is more knowledgeable. If you're chairing a meeting, try opening up the conversation to the group to ensure everyone's voice is heard. Asking directly by saying phrases like "We haven't heard from _____ in a bit. What do you think?" makes speaking easier for those who are usually spoken over or ignored.

CHANGEMAKERS

At a young age, Kailash Satyarthi realized that not all children living in India had the same opportunities he had. Many children lived in poverty and weren't able to attend school because they had to work to support their families. When he got older, Kailash used his privilege to fight child labor. He has led the rescue of tens of thousands of children forced to work in factories and given them the opportunity to get an education. Kailash also created a movement to raise awareness about child labor around the world. His activism led to the passing of a UN convention to prohibit child labor. In 2014, Kailash was awarded the Nobel Peace Prize along with Malala Yousafzai for their work on children's rights. Great activist company to be in!

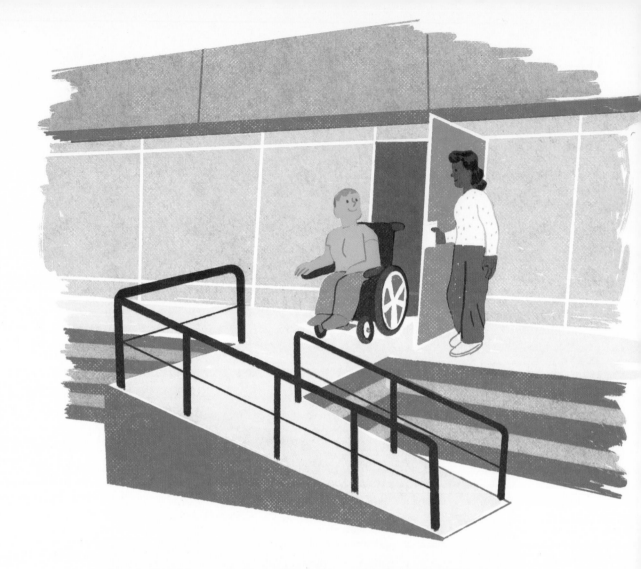

MAKING ACTIVISM ACCESSIBLE

To make social change, we need input from people with a wide range of perspectives and experiences. Captioning videos and photos, translating posters or holding events in accessible buildings are just some of the ways of welcoming and encouraging a diverse group of people to get involved.

CREATING SAFE SPACES

Once, after I gave a speech at a climate strike, a man approached me. He seemed friendly and told me that he was surprised I was so involved because I "didn't look like an activist." His comment made me uncomfortable. Later, I wondered if it was a microaggression, a subtle action of discrimination. Was the man implying that as a person of color, I didn't look like an activist — or didn't belong there? How did he form this idea of what an activist should look like? Does climate activism need to be more inclusive?

Creating safe spaces is essential to ensuring that everyone feels comfortable participating. It is also important to acknowledge that we ourselves may be guilty of microaggressions. If someone is offended by a comment you've made, hear them out, accept responsibility, apologize sincerely and do better in the future. If someone on your team says something offensive, address the issue. Your movement needs to be safe and inclusive for everyone.

DEALING WITH MICROAGGRESSIONS

Microaggressions are subtle, indirect interactions — either accidental or intentional — that convey a bias toward a marginalized group. Telling a person of color they speak English well, making statements about girls being naturally good at cooking and cleaning, saying a trans person doesn't "look transgender" — all of these are microaggressions.

How should you handle a microaggression?

- If you don't know the individual who made the comment, calling out the comment may do more harm than good. In this case, your action might be to console the person or people targeted by the comment. Follow up on how they're feeling and, if possible, discuss the comment openly in the group! "The individual who made this comment wanted to harm people in our group and we will not tolerate this discrimination."

- If the individual is part of your network, closely related to your cause or seems open to change, you may want to consider calmly critiquing their statement. You could speak to them immediately after they've made the comment or follow up later.

- To maintain a safe space within your group, you want others to know that you will take action against any discrimination they may face.

Let's consider an example: During a team meeting, you overhear one team member telling another that he is surprised they were able to write the press release in "fluent English." The person he was addressing is bilingual and speaks English with an accent. Here's how you could handle the microaggression:

1. **Ask the person who made the comment to reflect on it.** This gives the individual an opportunity to recognize the microaggression themselves. For example: "When you said that you were surprised they could write fluently, what did you mean by that?"

2. **Explain the issue. Let them know why that comment was wrong.** For example: "Although you meant to compliment them, your comment isolates our team member and implies that it's surprising that someone bilingual could write well in English. Even if this wasn't your intention, your words can still cause harm."

3. **Give an example. Offering an alternative way to give feedback will help them to improve.** For example: "Next time, you can just congratulate them on a job well done!"

RIPPLE EFFECT: an interview with
HANNAH CROUSE (she/her), COMMUNITY ACTIVIST

Hannah Crouse, then a student at Mount Allison University in New Brunswick, realized that many senior citizens were very isolated during the first COVID-19 lockdown in 2020. Hannah wanted to do something to help — and she thought other young activists would want to help, too. She put a call out on social media asking students if they would be interested in being paired with a senior in their community. Hannah was flooded with responses from eager allies. And the Community Connect program was born — and continues to grow.

How did you get interested in volunteering with seniors?

I was doing an internship at a health center in New Brunswick. Because of COVID restrictions, I wasn't able to work with patients in the clinic, so I started helping out in the community. One of my jobs was delivering food and tomato plants to seniors in the area. I started chatting with them and realized how lonely they were. I knew they really needed help and to see more people — and now! So I came up with the idea of the Community Connect project, pairing seniors with a student buddy.

What feedback have you received about the program?

The Community Connect project has been extremely mutually beneficial. The students went in thinking they wanted to do this to help out the seniors. But they came out of the experience saying they got much more out of the program than they could have imagined — that the seniors did more for them than they did for the seniors. Almost all the students want to continue volunteering in the program. And the seniors loved it! Some said they were hesitant to sign up for the program because they felt embarrassed to ask for "a friend." But after they joined, they said it was the best thing they could have done and told their friends to sign up. Through word of mouth, the program continues to grow. From a start of 18 students and 20 seniors, we now have more than 65 volunteers and 65 seniors in the program.

What advice do you have for young activists?

Remember, nothing is too small and nothing is too big. Getting involved can be draining, especially when your advocacy work is based around a personal piece of your identity. As a queer person, I can sometimes find the youth-based 2SLGBTQIA+ work exhausting. You feel like you are telling someone to respect a basic human right. So you need to do what works for you — and if it's a small action, that's okay. At the same time, don't be afraid to tackle big projects. If you can think it, you can do it. If you get discouraged, remind yourself of who you're doing it for and why you chose to do it. That will give you the energy and the fire to keep going. And don't assume you know what the community needs. Listen to the community and bring the community in as an equal partner, working together for a common goal.

NOBODY'S PERFECT

Saying you're an ally is much easier than being one. It's a process full of mistakes, reeducation and growth. Sometimes you will feel uncomfortable, challenged and hurt, and you will make mistakes. Taking a step back to reflect on your actions can help you assess and critique your approach and learn from your mistakes. Accepting constructive criticism is essential to this growth. If you know something you said is incorrect or you're not sure how to answer a question, just apologize or say you don't know.

Sometimes, in their efforts to support a cause, people may make mistakes. Remember that if you're a member of a marginalized group, it's not your job to educate others about your experiences. Your own mental health and well-being comes first. But if you want to help educate a supporter, these strategies may be helpful:

Politely explain the error they're making. If you feel safe doing so, explaining how they've made you or others uncomfortable can prevent the issue from coming up again. Your constructive feedback may spark a productive conversation!

Ask for help. If you don't feel comfortable criticizing someone's behavior (which is totally fine!), let a trusted adult know and ask for their help in deciding how to address the situation.

End the encounter. Sometimes, teammates can cause unintentional harm. If you're feeling unsafe or uncomfortable or need time to yourself, acknowledge those feelings and respond accordingly. Excuse yourself from the conversation so you have some time to recover. Consider reaching out to talk to someone about the situation.

BE A
CHANGEMAKER

You understand your privilege. You are committed to using your privilege and power to help others.

You stand in solidarity with others. You listen and learn, offering your skills and resources to support people and movements that have been marginalized, silenced or ignored.

You learn from your mistakes. You reflect on your actions and words, seeing them as an opportunity for learning.

6

LEAD

It was my first year of high school. My first school club. The first meeting of the Alliance for Compassion team — my school's 2SLGBTQIA+ rights and education group. I was so excited! I was passionate about raising awareness of issues affecting the 2SLGBTQIA+ community. But when I walked into the room, my heart fell. Aside from a couple of teacher moderators, only two other students were there.

I thought about walking away. Instead, I stepped up as team leader. Although I had a lot to learn about the 2SLGBTQIA+ community, I knew that it was an important issue in my school. I would often hear slurs and inappropriate jokes being made in the hallways and classrooms. Many students faced discrimination and were afraid to disclose their sexual orientation or gender identity for fear of harassment. Because of a lack of education, their peers were being thoughtlessly cruel. I began presenting to classes to let them know about the Alliance for Compassion and our meetings.

Slowly, more students began getting involved. We started initiatives like fundraisers to raise money for unhoused 2SLGBTQIA+ youth in Toronto. And we ran educational workshops at our school to teach about discrimination and foster allyship. Through it all, I tried to create a space where each team member felt comfortable to be themselves and allow their unique skills to shine. Together, we celebrated each success — big or small — and planned party days to appreciate everyone's hard work! I'm so proud of the team and what we accomplished.

IT TAKES A VILLAGE

To make social change, you need to work with others. And to work with others, you need to be organized. As your ideas for your cause move from concept to reality, think about what leadership model will work best to meet your goals. Co-leadership might be the best choice, or you might decide to go with a hierarchical model — with one leader in charge. Maybe a decentralized organization with no leaders will work best. The important thing is that everyone in the group is clear about the structure.

HOW TO ... LEAD

A leader is someone who guides people to achieve a common goal. Anyone with passion and drive can fulfill this role! Just follow these guidelines:

- Communicate your goals clearly and honestly.
- Think creatively to solve problems in innovative ways.
- Collaborate with others and understand everyone's capabilities.
- Take accountability for your actions and learn to resolve problems.
- Be positive and uplift others!

WHICH LEADERSHIP MODEL IS RIGHT FOR YOU?

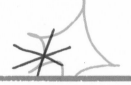

Co-leadership: Power is distributed among several people who fill different roles. Decisions are made by all co-leaders. Sweetest example: Ben & Jerry's ice cream was actually started by two activists named Ben and Jerry!

Hierarchical: Everyone reports to one leader. The leader has the authority and responsibility to make decisions. When Blake Mycoskie started TOMS, a footwear and clothing company, he decided to donate a pair of shoes to a child in a developing country each time one of their products was purchased. And under Mycoskie's leadership, the business became a socially conscious success.

Decentralized: No leaders at all. Look no further than Monarch Watch. Governments and citizen scientist volunteers in the United States, Canada and Mexico participate in this nonprofit program, working together to track the fall migration of the endangered monarch butterfly, collect data and protect its habitat across North America.

CHANGEMAKERS

At a time when few women in her town in Kenya even had the opportunity to learn to read, Wangari Maathai won a scholarship to attend university in the United States and completed a master's degree in biology. When she returned home, she saw how deforestation was hurting Kenya. For decades, British colonists had cut down trees to use the land to grow tea, coffee and tobacco. Now, Kenyans had achieved independence but the devastating practices continued. Streams were drying up, wildlife was gone and women had to walk farther to find firewood for fuel and cooking. Wangari knew she had to act. In 1977, she started the Green Belt Movement to replant trees in Kenya and to fight for women's rights and democracy. She raised money to start tree nurseries where women were paid to grow seedlings and plant trees in deforested areas. Although Wangari was imprisoned many times for fighting the authoritarian government's policies, she didn't give up. Thanks to her vision and determination, more than 51 million trees have been planted in Kenya.

WHAT KIND OF **TEAM MEMBER** ARE YOU?

What skills and passions do you bring to your initiative? What roles and responsibilities should you take on? This quiz will help you decide!

Your local cat shelter recently welcomed 20 new cats! You're volunteering to help raise money for their veterinary bills and have gathered a team to help. What kind of expertise do you have?

---

1. **You shine on a team and are great at collaborating and communicating with others. One of your team members wants to run a car wash for the fundraiser and another wants to hold a talent show. Your team begins disagreeing and losing sight of the overall goal. What should you do?**

a) You try to mediate the situation by reminding your teammates of the importance of collaboration.

Now that your group is getting along again, you have some great news to share. A local politician has heard about your event and wants to attend to help fundraise! How will you thank them?

i) *You'll greet them by the door and ensure they're feeling welcomed.*

Friendly Networker: Simply put ... you're a people person! You know the best way to build your movement is to build your community. You're great at reaching out to organizations, advertising through social media and planning events with others.

ii) *When you're doing your event's kick-off speech, you'll give them a kind shout-out.*

Spotlight Speaker: You love public speaking and don't mind being the center of attention. Whenever your team needs a volunteer for interviews, speeches or communicating with other activists, you're up for the task!

b) You create a pros and cons list for each of the ideas.

Deciding on the car wash, you all begin preparing for your big event. However, an hour before the event, you are faced with a huge problem ... your microphone isn't working! What do you do?

i) *You ask someone for help. Maybe they know how to fix it!*

Big-Picture Specialist: As a realistic thinker, you're able to see your initiatives through a wider scope. You ensure all rules and safety regulations are followed.

ii) *You volunteer to fix it. That's your kind of fun!*

Troubleshooting Expert: There's no job you can't do. You are a versatile, well-rounded quick learner. Your excellent problem-solving skills ensure no gadget stumps you!

c) You decide to hold a social for your team to focus on building relationships.

Mountain Mover: You keep a smile on everyone's face by motivating and uplifting spirits. By ensuring everyone is on task, staying positive and having fun, you are the heart of every team.

2. You love thinking outside the box and are known for your bright, creative mind. Now, you need to raise awareness about your fundraiser. What do you work on?

a) You post on all kinds of social media accounts so your network knows about the event.

> **Marketing Master:** You have a knack for staying on message and making an impact. You're great with social media and know the right caption for every occasion.

b) You put up flyers around the community and use word of mouth to tell your friends and family!
When creating these flyers, how do you prefer helping?

> **i)** *You come up with funny slogans that will catch attention.*
>
> **Writing Wizard:** You have a way with words. Your creative articles, bios, blogs and more keep others engaged!

> **ii)** *You come up with a color theme and create the graphics to go on the poster.*
>
> **Creative Thinker:** You're known for your ability to create strong visual messages. Your initiatives stand out and constantly challenge the norm.

3. You're extremely organized and would love to help plan the event. Your team has decided to plan a car wash for your fundraiser. Which role do you take on?

a) You budget for the supplies needed and estimate your profit.

> **Number Cruncher:** Math is one of your best subjects in school and you love all things numbers! You're responsible for budgeting and dealing with your team's finances.

b) You research car washes and discover your local climate group ran one last year. You reach out and ask them for tips.

> **Reliable Researcher:** You rely on resources to help you find an answer. You're skilled at finding trustworthy facts and communicating this information to the group.

c) You keep the team on track by creating a calendar of important tasks and deadlines.

> **Planning Pro:** You always know what's happening and when. Your amazing sense of time keeps the team on track.

BUILDING A
DREAM TEAM

Sometimes a group forms quickly and organically — a group of classmates discover a shared passion or a post-protest conversation develops among strangers. But often you need to hold a general interest meeting to recruit members. If that's the case, you can make posters and use social media to get the word out. And do some thinking about how you imagine that group working together. What work will the group be doing? What different leadership roles will need to be filled? What skills or expertise will be needed? Will you need additional volunteers? How will you make sure your marginalized participants feel safe and welcome? Make time to consider these questions before you begin recruiting. It will pay off down the road.

RIPPLE EFFECT: an interview with
ISABELA RITTINGER (she/her), MENSTRUAL JUSTICE ACTIVIST

When the COVID-19 pandemic began in 2020, people started stockpiling period products. Isabela Rittinger was upset about how this was affecting people who were already struggling to access and afford tampons and pads. So she quickly got to work, connecting with other youth to create Bleed the North. The organization continues to fight to end period poverty and period stigma.

Why did you start Bleed the North?

Even before the pandemic, one in three menstruators under the age of 25 couldn't afford period products. So when I heard about people stockpiling period products, I was upset by the impact this panic-buying was having on people who were already struggling to get access to and cover the costs of tampons and pads. I put out a call to action on Instagram to my friends and school community asking them to help provide period products to those in need. Only five people attended the first meeting. But we were keen. We got to work spreading the word on social media, asking for contactless donations of period products. My mom and I drove around the area picking up donations and dropping them off at shelters.

What was the most challenging part for you?

The toughest part was figuring out a good organizational structure. From five people at our first meeting, we've grown to an organization with more than 110 members. I soon realized that I couldn't do this on my own, so we formed an executive team based on the three pillars of the organization: Service (to provide menstrual products), Education (to provide resources on period poverty and stigma) and Advocacy (to work for menstrual equity). This co-leadership model allows us to get more volunteers involved in a meaningful way, develop new initiatives and partnerships, and reach our collective goals.

What advice do you have for young activists?

Surround yourself with people you trust. Set collective goals and stay focused on them. Make space for others to develop their leadership skills. And remember, you're always learning. When we started the organization, we used the term "feminine" hygiene products. In working to create a safe and inclusive space and listening to nonbinary and trans members, we've disassociated our language from gender to be clear that Bleed the North supports everyone who menstruates.

To learn more about Bleed the North, visit www.bleedthenorth.org.

ALL IN A
DAY'S WORK

As a leader, you play many different roles. Sometimes, you need to be fun and energetic to uplift the group's spirits. Sometimes, you may be hard at work researching organizations. When you're answering emails, talking to a politician or meeting a donor, you'll need to adopt a more professional manner. Many people will underestimate you because you're young. Challenge their preconceptions. Avoid using slang, try talking in full sentences and support your position with facts. And use your leadership tool kit to stay organized, constructive and safe!

ORGANIZATION MATTERS

Leadership comes with a ton of responsibility — you may find it hard to keep track of everything! Emails, deadlines, phone numbers and names can all get jumbled up and easily lost. Keep all key information organized in a system that works for you.

While I've shared strategies that work for me, they might not work for you. You'll find your own system of organization. Maybe you fill out a planner for every month, keep all your important documents online or create color-coded lists. Try out different organizational tools until you find the ones that suit you best.

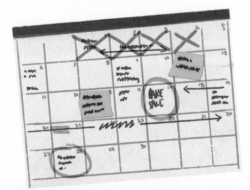

TIPS FROM A PRO

I keep a huge calendar with all of my important school, volunteer, work and activism dates. This way, I'm able to plan my time while taking all of my commitments into consideration. When I see on my calendar that my sister's birthday is on the weekend *and* I have a test the following Monday, I make sure to do my activism work beforehand.

I love making a daily to-do list. This keeps me focused — and more productive. Be careful that you don't overestimate what you can complete. Make sure your list is doable in a day.

I'm constantly improving my workspace. I imagine I'm entering my workspace as a stranger. Would I understand what tasks need to be done? Would I be able to find contact information? Would I know how everything works? When you're collaborating with others and need to share information quickly, it's important for everything to be crystal clear. Something that makes sense to you may be confusing for others.

MEET UP

There may be times when your leadership role includes chairing a meeting. Whether you're handling this by yourself or with others, preparation is key to calming nerves!

Start by thinking about your goal for the meeting. Is it an update, announcement, brainstorming session, introduction, training or something else? This will help you decide whether the meeting should be more formal (you do most of the talking and allow attendees to ask questions afterward) or collaborative (you guide conversations as an equal member). Also, think about the other roles that you might need people to take on, such as notetaker.

HOW TO ...
ORGANIZE A MEETING

- Find an accessible location.
- Invite people: Share information about the cause and action. Provide a date, time and location. List a contact person and their info.
- Create an agenda of speakers for each important topic and allot a realistic amount of time for each.
- Start the meeting off by introducing yourself, stating your pronouns, offering a land acknowledgment and then reviewing the agenda.
- Keep track of action items during the meeting.
- Close the meeting with a quick review to make sure people know what they have to do.

TIP:
Icebreakers are a great way to help people feel more comfortable before the discussion begins. My favorite is "two truths and a lie." In this icebreaker, each person shares two truths and a lie about themselves and the group has to guess which is the lie.

CHANGEMAKERS

In 2001, Reverend Dr. Brent Hawkes officiated at the first legally recognized same-sex marriage in the world in Toronto, Ontario. At the time, gay marriage was still illegal in Canada and city clerks would not issue marriage licenses for same-sex marriages. Hawkes used the alternative allowed under provincial law — to publish official banns (public announcements) of marriage for three weeks before the ceremony. Hawkes received death and bomb threats and had to wear a bulletproof vest to the ceremony, but it was worth it to change the course of 2SLGBTQIA+ history. Just two years later, same-sex marriage became legal in Ontario.

EVERYONE'S A
CRITIC

As a leader, it's your responsibility to make sure that those who generously volunteer their time understand that every task, no matter how seemingly small and insignificant, is important. And it's up to you to make it clear what you need volunteers to do. Sometimes you'll need to offer constructive feedback. You don't want to hurt anyone's feelings ... especially after they've put in a lot of time and effort for the cause. Remember that you're critiquing the work and not the person.

Listening to constructive criticism from volunteers is important, too. It's an opportunity to grow as a leader. When someone approaches you with a suggestion or request, welcome their idea with an open mind. Did you make a mistake? Could you improve in this area? As a leader, you need to be flexible and responsive to your team members' needs — and to do that, you need their honest feedback. Remember, they're critiquing the work ... not you!

THE SANDWICH METHOD

So how do you give constructive feedback in an appropriate, sensitive way? Serve up the sandwich method.

THE BUN
Begin with a positive statement about a strength of their work or an aspect you enjoyed. "Hey! Your press release title is so good. I love how catchy it is, it definitely gave me a laugh."

THE FILLING
Focus on how the work could be improved, but stay positive. "Could you try rewording some of the sentences in the main paragraph to be more concise and direct? That way, the media will be able to skim through the press release quickly. I can help you if you'd like!"

THE BUN
Finish off with a compliment. "Overall, the press release is attention-grabbing and well-written. Great job!"

SAFETY FIRST

As a leader, you are responsible for ensuring all events, meetings and initiatives are safe for your teammates and everyone involved. That can be as straightforward as making sure that everyone feels welcome at a meeting or as complex as arranging safe protests. Always start preparing by thinking about what will happen at the event — and what could go wrong. What can you do to avoid problems? What resources do you need to keep people safe? If unexpected emergencies come up, have a plan and the necessary resources at hand. Relying on a trusted adult to advise and support you is extremely important — especially if you are finding that an event is a lot to deal with on your own.

When I organized a walkout at my school to protest education budget cuts, I thought about what could go wrong and how I would handle it. What if someone got hurt during the march? What if a few students got into a fight? What if someone left the school property? Because I wasn't able to watch every single person, I asked some teachers to attend to troubleshoot and jump in to help resolve issues. And before the walkout, we explained our goals to students and how they would need to behave to participate — and keep themselves and their peers safe.

CREATING SAFE SPACES AT MEETINGS

- Choose accessible meeting spaces.
- Identify if you need interpreters, including American Sign Language.
- Give people the option of sharing their preferred pronouns.
- Make sure only one person speaks at a time and people don't interrupt or have side conversations.
- Make it clear that private information shared at the meeting should not be shared outside the group.
- If disagreements arise, remind people of the rules for speaking — and listening. If tempers are still flaring, take a break so people can cool down.

BE A
CHANGEMAKER

You choose the best leadership model for your organization. You understand that the leadership model you choose depends on your goals and situation.

You build a team based on your needs and goals. You recruit and inspire people with the skills and passion needed for your cause.

You understand and use leadership tools. By staying organized, constructive and safe, you lead your team and movement to success.

7

YOU GOT
THIS

The first time I printed a little robot with my library's brand-new 3D printer, I was hooked. I discovered I loved tinkering around with new machines and decided to take a robotics class at school. When I walked into the room, I was shocked. I was the only girl in the class! I started second-guessing my decision to study robotics. I felt weird and wondered if I belonged there. *What if I'm not smart enough to take these classes? What if I can't make friends? Am I the only one finding this difficult?* Sometimes I even felt anxious going to class. There was no reason for me to doubt my ability to do well in the class — but I did. After befriending some of my classmates, I learned I was not alone in finding it difficult. Eventually, I found community in my classroom and became confident in my abilities. I was as capable as anyone else and I deserved to be there. Even though I still feel those insecurities sometimes, I remind myself of my strengths. Everyone faces challenges and it's okay to struggle — what's important is that we keep persisting!

STARING DOWN
SELF-DOUBT

It's normal to be nervous when you're thrown into a challenging new situation. But you shouldn't feel like a fraud. If the voice in your head is telling you that you only succeeded because of luck and you aren't as skilled as others think you are, you're not alone.

- Share your feelings.
- Separate your feelings from the facts.
- Think about why you may be doubting yourself.
- Focus on the positive.
- Realize you have the right to make a mistake.
- Learn from failure.
- Change the conversation in your head.
- Visualize your successes. Celebrate them when they happen.
- Be courageous. Confidence will come.

CLEARING THE HURDLES

No social justice initiative is simple or smooth sailing. If activism were easy, these issues wouldn't be as prominent as they are today. All leaders face hurdles on the way to success. Especially when you're trying something new, it's common for doubt to creep in. But when your activism isn't as successful as you'd hoped, it's an opportunity to build resilience and creative-thinking skills. By staying confident in yourself and your abilities, you will find your goals easier to achieve. Whatever the obstacles, you'll find a way to work around them. Whether it's the sting of a rude comment, an unsuccessful campaign for policy change or a failed fundraising event — all setbacks I've faced — you can recover and grow in your activism.

BEWARE OF TROLLS

Social media is a great tool for activism. But it's also a place where people can hide behind anonymous profiles to make hurtful comments. I know because I've experienced it. After a long day of climate striking, I was excited to share my photos and experiences online. When I checked my feed the next day, my heart sank. Someone called me a terrorist in a comment. Even though I knew this comment was untrue and just spewing hatred, it still hurt to read it. I felt as if my hard work had gone unnoticed and that my skin color was all that people saw. Although I was upset, I remembered my reason for striking — to protect our planet. I wasn't going to let a comment like this stop me. I blocked the account, put my phone away for the day and talked to some friends about it. Then I continued with my activism, more committed than ever!

HOW TO ...
DEAL WITH HURTFUL COMMENTS

1. **Remember, the haters just want attention!** So don't give it to them. Don't let the comment bring you down — and keep fighting for your cause!

2. **Tell a trusted adult about the comment.** You'll feel better. Plus, they'll have ideas on how to deal with the problem appropriately.

3. **Report it!** If this comment was made on social media, report the user. Block online trolls and delete their comments! If the comment came from a student or someone you know, an adult can report it to their school for further action.

These hurtful insults may take time to recover from, but they are not your story. Use them to strengthen your commitment to your cause!

TOUGH CONVERSATIONS

While many people will want to learn about your cause and engage in constructive conversations, some people will not be open to new ideas. When faced with someone who refuses to consider your opinion, the best response is to focus your energies elsewhere. But if the individual is a family member, politician or teacher — someone important to you or to your community — keep the lines of communication open. Continue to discuss this social justice topic with them. You'll both learn from your conversations! Remember to maintain respect and a level head so these productive discussions don't turn into heated arguments. While these conversations can be extremely constructive for both parties, your emotional well-being comes first!

HOW TO ...
DISAGREE PRODUCTIVELY

Not everyone will understand your position on social justice issues. When they challenge your activism, stay calm and respond. Here's an example:

"I don't understand why you advocate for those who are unhoused in our city. They should just get jobs or leave!"

1. **Acknowledge that you have heard their statement.** "I see why you would think that, but we don't know every person's individual story and history."

2. **Explain your outlook concisely.** "There are many reasons why someone can become unhoused and many barriers preventing them from getting out of their situation."

3. **Give an example.** "Getting a job while unhoused isn't easy. Most employers require that you have a mailing address, and so, if you're unhoused, you aren't even able to apply."

4. **Explain why their outlook is flawed.** "By putting the blame on those who are unhoused, we're avoiding looking at the systemic issues, such as poverty and lack of support for mental health, that contribute to the problem."

5. **Explain how your outlooks may come from the same perspective.** "I do agree that we should be increasing job availability! However, we need to provide unhoused people with the right resources so they are able to make this transition."

RESPECT YOURSELF

As an activist, you will face those who question why they should listen to you or care about what you have to say. This can be very intimidating. When I put forward the motion in support of the declaration of a climate emergency, I could sense that the councillors didn't respect me as much as they respected their fellow adults. They made comments like "That's so inspiring" and "Good for you," rather than asking me detailed questions like they did the adult delegates. However, I knew I was well-informed and that they would benefit from learning about this youth movement. I stayed confident, earning their respect with a well-researched presentation. Recognize your own skills and use them to the best of your ability. When you understand and are proud of your contributions, the opinions of others are less intimidating. Your strengths will shine through.

CHANGEMAKERS

The Craftivist Collective uses a kinder, nonconfrontational approach to activism. For their Don't Blow It campaign, which urged UK retailer Marks & Spencer to raise workers' salaries above minimum wage, they got creative. Volunteers hand-stitched positive, personal messages on a hankie for each board member, stating why paying a living wage was good for business. Then, each hankie was wrapped and given to the appropriate board member at the company's annual general meeting. Craftivists also had "stitch-ins" outside Marks & Spencer stores across the UK to encourage customers and staff to let the company know if they supported raising wages. And thanks to this kind campaign, 50 000 employees' wages were increased.

RIPPLE EFFECT: an interview with
NATHANIEL LUCES (he/him), ANTI-BLACK RACISM ACTIVIST

After the murder of George Floyd, Nathaniel, like many others, wanted to do something to fight anti-Black racism. He got involved with Break the Chains Pickering, an organization raising awareness about anti-Black racism in policing, education and employment systems. And that was just the beginning!

What was it like speaking at your first protest?

I was terrified! I had never done anything like that. But it was amazing. It got me out of my comfort zone. I had so much self-doubt. *Is my speech going to be good or cringey?* Being around people who supported and encouraged me was really helpful. They reminded me to focus on speaking from the heart. Just saying what's truly on my mind. I spoke about something I feel passionately about — the need to incorporate Black history in the curriculum. So much of identity is based on understanding who we are. But my history is not represented in the curriculum. I talked about how history is more complicated and dynamic than the European and colonist experience. Everything started to happen after that speech. People in the community knew who I was. Opportunities and doorways opened up. I was even invited to become part of the Brothers United Mentorship Program for Black youth ages 10–14. Working with youth was something I had always wanted to do.

What hurdles have you faced?

After the Break the Chains demonstration, I was asked to speak at city council. They were proud to see youth in the community taking a stand and wanted to engage further. It was a perfect opportunity for our team to educate the council on the issues and make recommendations. We researched and wrote proposals for actions, including the creation of an anti-Black racism committee chaired by people from the Black community. But the answer was no. We were angry. We were upset. Some people were discouraged. For me, I realized that in this fight, you're going to get a lot of nos. You're going to face a lot of pushback. You're going to get a lot of indirect answers. You have to stand firm. And keep fighting for the change you want to see. So I became a co-leader of our school's Unity/Black History Committee. We made proposals to the school board for how to address the racism that Black students faced. Again, our recommendations were ignored. As disappointing as it was, hope gave me strength to keep pushing. It became my superpower.

What advice do you have for young activists?

You are not just a label to be put in a box. You have the potential to become many other things. You have the capacity to make a significant change. Believe in yourself. Use your creativity. A lot of youth may feel like imposters — that they aren't really doing anything significant or important. That was my experience. It's so important that you don't doubt yourself and your abilities. Being underestimated by adults gives you the time and space to plan the changes you really want to see. Sometimes it's not even something you realize is possible until you see the change happen. It's not until the people around you say, "Oh, this helped this person in this way" or "This initiative led to this result" that you realize what you are capable of.

GOING THE
DISTANCE

People who believe their talents can be developed through hard work, good strategies and the guidance of others are said to have a growth mindset. Obstacles are viewed as thought-provoking opportunities. In contrast, those with fixed mindsets believe they're born with their talents and nothing is going to change them. When they face an obstacle, they don't believe they can overcome it.

When you begin feeling discouraged, remind yourself of how much you've accomplished and grown already! Every step you take on your activism journey, every barrier you overcome, is worth celebrating. When I'm struggling and feeling frustrated, I look at pictures of climate strikes I've been to. When I see the dedication and passion in everyone's eyes, I'm reminded of why I got involved in activism and start feeling motivated again! By focusing on your overall purpose, you will realize the minor hassles aren't worth stressing over.

PACE YOURSELF

Social injustices arise from a complex web of issues that can't be solved overnight. Worrying about progress and taking on too much responsibility can lead to grief, obsessive thoughts, guilt, poor eating habits, difficulty sleeping and other symptoms of depression and anxiety.

Remember, you have no control over the actions of others. What you can control is what you do in response to setbacks. Your passion should fuel you to make change — not be a source of stress. If you're feeling overwhelmed by your cause, you're probably starting with initiatives that require more resources than you have. Try breaking your goals into smaller, more achievable chunks.

KEEP IT
REALISTIC

Discrimination was an issue in my high school. In response, my school's social justice student groups made a proposal to hold full-day anti-discrimination workshops for all students. Great idea, right? But we didn't have the resources or support to do it. Here's how we came up with creative solutions.

1. **Identify the issues.** Teachers would not agree to let students out of class for anti-discrimination training. Plus, we didn't have enough volunteers to run these workshops.

2. **Brainstorm possible solutions.** We could cut down the presentation to just 30 minutes! We talked with other students and figured out that slurs and language use were a major issue at our school. Rather than touching on every form of discriminatory behavior, we focused on these two.

3. **Focus your efforts.** We also decided to address only the 10th and 11th grade students. Our survey indicated they exhibited and experienced higher levels of discrimination and needed the workshops the most.

CHANGEMAKERS

When Winona LaDuke was 18 years old, she addressed the United Nations for the first time, providing expert testimony about the environmental impact of mining on Indigenous lands. LaDuke soon became an internationally respected environmental leader. Now, more than 40 years later, she continues to advocate for environmental issues and Indigenous rights and to inspire the next generation to continue the fight.

TAKE
CARE

TRY A LITTLE POSITIVITY

Try using affirmation statements when self-doubt starts to creep in. They'll help you to see things in a more positive light and remind you of your core values — and why you're doing what you're doing. And with all those positive vibes flowing, you may be more open to changing your behavior to help you achieve your goals. An affirmation can be delivered in many ways: speaking to yourself in the mirror, writing down your successes, acknowledging your improvements or celebrating your abilities!

If you find that you're being overly critical of yourself, take five minutes to test out one of these affirmation statements:

- I can do this.
- I will try again, even if it's tough.
- I do not worry about things that are out of my control.
- I am thankful for everything I have.
- I can create change.
- I am loved.
- I can inspire others.
- I am a leader.
- I learn from my challenges.
- I am proud of myself.
- My voice and opinions matter.

TRUST YOURSELF

Confidence is a belief in oneself — not an emotion. Our confidence affects how we react in situations, talk to others and feel about ourselves. Having a realistic sense of our abilities and the confidence that we can handle challenges helps us to deal with pressure.

Even if we think we're confident, we can experience self-doubt. In my robotics class, I noticed that I was apologizing for "making mistakes" that weren't even mistakes! We were encouraged to experiment with hardware and, if I didn't get it right the first time, I felt bad and apologized. Now, I stop and think before I speak to avoid making statements that downplay my abilities. Instead of saying, "Sorry, I'm really bad at this," I say, "I don't have much experience with this. Do you have any advice?"

When you believe in yourself, you can hold your head high, rely on yourself for reassurance and know that any hurdles you may face are a product of your situation — not you!

LISTEN TO YOUR BODY

Your activism will be the most effective when you're taking care of yourself and others. Remember to take breaks so you don't burn out from overwork or too much stress. When you find yourself feeling stressed and exhausted, your body's telling you to take time to yourself.

If you're feeling stressed, ask yourself these questions:

- Have I been drinking water?
- Have I eaten healthy foods?
- Have I gotten enough sleep? Am I energized?
- Have I completed other, more time-sensitive tasks or chores?
- Have I taken a break recently?
- Am I feeling better?

If you haven't answered yes to all these questions, take a break! Go outside, chat with your friends and family, read a book, paint a picture and put your mental health *first*!

BE A
CHANGEMAKER

You face obstacles but continue to persevere. You see challenges as an opportunity to learn.

You realize you can overcome setbacks. You make time to celebrate your successes and to make sure your initiatives are achievable.

You develop strategies for caring for yourself. You understand that activists risk burning out, so you implement good practices.

8

YOUR ACTIVISM
JOURNEY

After being involved in social justice initiatives for a few years, I was ready to take my activism in a new direction. I thought more and more about my career path. I was curious about technology and coding and wondered if I could combine this new interest with why I wanted to get involved in activism in the first place — to fight for justice in my community.

I heard about a new group called the e-NABLE Toronto team, the first student-led Canadian chapter of a global community of "Digital Humanitarian" volunteers. The organization uses 3D printers to make free and low-cost prosthetic upper-limb devices for children and adults in need. The group sounded super cool, so I decided to go to the first meeting. And I signed up! I loved that I could acquire new tech skills while helping others. I learned how to use 3D printers, assemble prosthetics and even create my own designs. In my second year, I took over as the leader of the group, training and directing our volunteers, solving design errors, coordinating with recipients of our prosthetics, managing social media and fundraising to finance our initiative. This initiative was more complex than many others I had joined, as I needed to build lots of technical skills to be able to support team members. But it was perfect for me and has inspired me to work with technology and robots in my future career.

TO THE
FUTURE
AND
BEYOND

As you grow as an individual, your passions, interests and strengths will change and grow with you. Rather than making activism a thing of your past, you can adapt your advocacy to fit your current goals and future plans.

Think back to why you wanted to be an activist in the first place. Before you got caught up with organizing campaigns and chairing meetings, why did you want to get involved? Who did you want to help? Why was the issue meaningful to you? What's changed? What's the same? Throughout it all, what's kept you motivated?

As an activist, you need the support of your friends, family members, teachers and peers to bolster your enthusiasm and help you to meet your goals. Whether your loved ones are actively involved with the issue or not, it's their support that helps you to stay positive and pursue your passions. But your motivation doesn't have to come just from a person ... it can be anything that inspires you and fills you with energy! For me, it's news stories about other people's successes in activism. They lift me up and remind me that activists make significant impacts — and I can, too!

ONE STEP AT A TIME

Activism is not easy. And it takes time. Remember that real change doesn't come quickly — it comes from dedication and a series of small, thoughtful actions. Don't be discouraged if your individual actions seem inconsequential. It's not the biggest, showiest actions with the most media buzz that make a difference. Continue to work for effective, sustainable and consistent change. The small, strategic actions you're currently taking will have long-lasting effects. Remember, it's better to have millions of people making an effort toward social change than thousands of people acting perfectly. Even something that seems small, such as bringing a mug to a fast-food restaurant, can have a big impact and save billions of cups from going into the landfill each year.

Most of all, remember to have fun! Instead of waiting to commemorate big, momentous achievements, celebrate every small step on your activism journey as its own accomplishment.

YOUR NEXT

KEEP HOPE ALIVE

If you're feeling that your activism plan isn't getting the results you want, try switching some things up. It's normal for your initial plans to shift and morph, inspiring new, creative approaches. When our Alliance for Compassion was trying to build 2SLGBTQIA+ awareness, we planned a fun quiz in the cafeteria to raise awareness of different identities. Sadly, no one showed up. Later, we realized there was a football game at the same time and, because we were late in our planning, we'd done a lousy job promoting the event. We were upset but took a deep breath and decided to try again. Next time, we checked that we weren't competing against other school activities, made sure the event was well advertised and added a prize incentive to encourage people to show up. Despite our setback, we reached our goal of fostering constructive conversations about the 2SLGBTQIA+ community and learned a valuable lesson about planning!

CHAPTER

BUILD A BIG TENT

After working in Ontario's Legislative Assembly as a page, I had a newfound interest in the government and how it can justly represent its citizens. At the time, I was also involved with my school's eco team and wondered if I could combine this with my interest in government policy. That led me to the climate movement! Talking to other climate strikers, I discovered that we got involved for various reasons. Some of my friends were passionate about protecting Indigenous rights, some cared about sustainable agriculture and some just wanted to protect nature and Earth's resources. We were inspired by different aspects of climate injustice but all had the same goals. I realized that the climate movement was much more complex than I had thought. There are many different perspectives to bring to an issue or problem.

All social justice issues are intertwined in some form. When fighting for one cause, you will find that it involves many others as well. Even though your focus may be in one area of advocacy, you can't help people without recognizing that their other identities contribute to the challenges they are facing. Once you've found a passion for a cause, try to think about how it involves other social justice issues, too. For example, the fight for gender equality must address racial injustices because racialized women are affected by both racial and gender discrimination. Creating activism plans that account for different perspectives — not just yours — will help you ensure your activism is long-lived and continues to grow.

INTERSECTIONALITY:

Intersectionality is a term coined by Black feminist scholar Kimberlé Crenshaw. It's a framework for understanding the ways people facing multiple forms of inequality and marginalization are disadvantaged. It helps us to understand how the obstacles they face may not be addressed by conventional ways of thinking about social inequities.

YES YOU CAN

When people first told me that I could change the world, I rolled my eyes. The idea that my actions could have such a drastic impact seemed very naive. Yet the more I get involved in the world of activism, the more I understand the truth in that statement.

You will never fully know the ripple effect of your activism and its impact on others' lives. Or how your fight for change inspires others. Or when your actions shift others' perspectives. Or how future generations will benefit from your work. But by getting involved and encouraging others to use their skills and talents for social justice, you'll expand your movements and make long-lasting changes in the world. Together, we can make activism the new norm! When we put our bright minds and creative talents together, there is no limit to what we can accomplish.

NEXT STEPS

Congratulations on completing *You Can Be an Activist*! Now, you're armed with skills and tools to help you begin your own activism journey and make a difference in your community and beyond.

If you're feeling unsure about how you can take that first step, don't worry — we've got you covered! Here are some ideas to get you started:

- **Look at the news:** Spend some time reviewing local and global news stories from the past month. Make a list of any social justice movements you read about or ideas for improving your community that the stories inspire.

- **Take a walk in your neighborhood:** Explore your community and take note of any issues or areas that need improvement. Do you see excessive litter, inaccessible public spaces or other concerns that catch your attention? Do you have ideas on how you could make positive change?

- **Talk to your friends and family:** Reach out to those who know you best. Brainstorming together can be a great way to identify social justice causes you feel passionate about.

- **Identify your skills:** Reflect on your own unique strengths and talents. How can you apply these to your activism? Review "You've Got What It Takes" on page 12.

- **Research organizations:** Look at local and national organizations and volunteer groups that align with your values and interests. These may be groups you can join or organizations that can help inspire your own campaign. Use the email template on page 23 to reach out to organizations.

- **Attend events:** Keep an eye out for events and activities being held within your communities. Rallies, protests and community gatherings are a great way to learn more about social justice issues and connect with other activists.

- **Learn more:** Continue to educate yourself on social justice issues and their history. Reading books, watching documentaries and researching reliable online resources are a great way to expand your knowledge.

- **Brainstorm your own initiative:** If you have a social justice issue in mind, refer to "What Action Is Right for Your Cause" on page 31 for ideas on how to spearhead your own activism movement.

Remember, every effort, no matter how small, makes a difference. So go out and take action. Become an agent of change — one step at a time!

Dear Reader,

We hope that this book has sparked thoughtful questions and inspirational conversations about what it means to make a difference.

Developed by Kids Can Press, the CitizenKid collection encourages young readers to learn about global issues and then think about ways that they can help improve the communities they live in, and the world at large.

Almost 2 million CitizenKid books have been sold to date, and the collection has been translated into over 25 languages. CitizenKid books have garnered worldwide critical acclaim.

Each CitizenKid book is developed with one or more of the United Nations Sustainable Development Goals (SDG) in mind, such as climate action, clean water and sanitation, gender equality, poverty and more. The Goals are a universal call to action to end poverty, protect the planet and improve the lives and prospects of everyone, everywhere.

For our part, Kids Can Press is a proud signatory of the UN's SDG Publisher's Compact. The Compact is designed to accelerate progress to achieve the Goals through publishing books that support positive change.

How will you help change the world?

#CitizenKid

ACKNOWLEDGMENTS

From the first spark of the idea, the goal of *You Can Be an Activist* was to inspire and support youth in making effective change. Throughout the process, we too have been inspired and bolstered in ways that made the book much richer than we could have imagined. Our sincere thanks to the changemakers who have gone before. To the young activists who shared their experiences in the book — Hannah Crouse, Mansoor Hussaini, Peyton Klein, Nathaniel Luces, Rae Paul, Isabela Rittinger and AnnaLee Rain Yellowhammer — your work, advice and inspiration is so valuable and deeply appreciated. Huge thanks to the talented team at Kids Can Press who believed in and nurtured this book with such care. Special thanks to our editor Kathleen Keenan for her keen eye and thoughtful guidance and to our extraordinary designer Andrew Dupuis for his creative vision. A much-deserved shout out to Anna Bendiy and Olga Kidisevic for piloting the project through production. And to Drew Shannon, our deepest thanks for your stunning artwork and for delighting us and readers. A heartfelt thanks to Charlene's family, Leilani, Nedenia and Cilbur Rocha, as well as Mary Beth's family, Jeff, Ben and Sarah Krymalowski, for their unwavering love and support throughout our own activism journeys. And to you, dear reader, thank you for your passion and commitment. The world needs you, and know we're here cheering you on.

— Charlene and Mary Beth

A NOTE FROM MARY BETH

When I was your age, I saw injustices in my community, but as a kid I didn't believe that I had the ability to do anything about them. Now I know I was wrong. Over the years, I've worked with many inspiring activists of all ages. They've taught me that there are many ways to support and effect change, and that using my skills and privilege as a writer and editor to elevate diverse voices and shine a light on social justice issues is, in fact, a form of quiet activism.

I'm glad you'll have this book by your side as you're figuring out how to use your strengths and talents to tackle injustice. Charlene's successes and challenges, tips and strategies will be a great resource. Still, you may become discouraged sometimes and feel that your efforts are small and inconsequential. But like the Changemakers in this book, and the young activists profiled in Ripple Effect interviews, you too can take actions in your school and community that will have a huge positive impact on other people's lives — and your own. I can't wait to read about your work as an activist one day soon!

— MBL

RESOURCES

Act Up https://actupny.com/
American Civil Liberties Union https://www.aclu.org/
Black Lives Matter https://blacklivesmatter.com/
Bleed the North https://www.bleedthenorth.org/
Canadian Museum for Human Rights https://humanrights.ca/
Community Connect program https://mta.ca/about/news/community
-connect-mon-03282022-1440
Craftivist Collective https://craftivist-collective.com/
Enabling the Future (e-NABLE) https://enablingthefuture.org/
Freedom Summer https://www.archives.gov/research/african-americans/vote
/freedom-summer
Fridays For Future https://fridaysforfuture.org/
Global Minds Initiative https://globalminds.world/
Green Belt Movement http://www.greenbeltmovement.org/
Honor the Earth https://honorearth.org/
Independent Living Movement https://haslonline.org/about
/history-of-the-independent-living-movement/
Kailash Satyarthi's Children's Foundation https://satyarthi.org.in/
NAACP https://naacp.org/
National Center for Civil and Human Rights https://www.civilandhumanrights.org/
National Women's History Museum https://www.womenshistory.org/
NDN Collective https://ndncollective.org/
Rainbow Faith and Freedom https://rainbowfaithandfreedom.org/
United Farm Workers https://ufw.org/
United Nations Sustainable Development Goals https://www.un.org
/sustainabledevelopment/sustainable-development-goals/
Youth Project https://youthproject.ns.ca/

GLOSSARY

activist: someone who stands up for their own rights and the rights of others, taking action to create social change that benefits other people and the planet

allyship: the state of helping or supporting other people who are part of a group that is treated badly or unfairly, even if you are not a member of that group. Allyship requires active listening, unlearning biases, building relationships and taking action.

artivist: someone who raises awareness and works to make social change through the creation of art

bias: personal opinions and prejudices that affect someone's judgment

BIPOC: an acronym that stands for Black, Indigenous, people of color

Black Lives Matter movement: a political and social movement with a focus on highlighting the racism, discrimination and racial inequity experienced by Black people

campaign: a plan of activities to achieve a goal (like bringing attention to a social justice cause)

child labor: children doing work that endangers their health and well-being and deprives them of the opportunity to attend school

Civil Rights Movement: a social movement for racial equality in the United States during the 1950s and 1960s

colonialism: when one country takes control of an area or another country and claims the land as its own, often while imposing its own cultural values on the people living there

conscious activism: a form of activism that involves thoughtfully considering your actions, such as what you eat, wear and buy, and the impact of those actions, as well as being open to changing your habits

discrimination: treating a person or group differently, in a worse way than you treat other people, because of their race, gender, sexuality, ability, etc.

eco-justice: a social movement fighting for a better environmental future for all

equality: when everyone has or gets the same as everyone else

equity: when everyone gets what is just and fair based on their needs

fundraising: raising money or collecting goods for a cause

gender identity: a person's own internal sense of self and their gender. It could be boy, girl, neither or both.

intersectionality: the ways that different aspects of our identities — race, socioeconomic status, gender, sexuality, ability — affect our experiences and the discrimination we face

marginalization: the discrimination and social disadvantages people experience because of race, gender identity, sexual orientation, age, ability, religion, immigration status, socioeconomic class and other factors

microaggressions: subtle, sometimes unintentional insults that are based on or perpetuate stereotypes

petition: a document with a statement or demand supported and signed by people

privilege: the social power and advantages some people are granted by society as members of a particular race, class, gender identity or other group

queer: a descriptive term sometimes used by people whose sexual identity is not heterosexual and/or whose gender identity is not cisgender

sexual orientation: a pattern of emotional, romantic, and/or physical attraction to members of the same or other genders

social justice: the belief that all people should have the same rights and opportunities

2SLGBTQIA+: an acronym for Two-Spirit, lesbian, gay, bisexual, transgender, queer or questing, intersex, asexual and additional sexual orientations and gender identities

INDEX